GENERATIVE A.I WITH

PYTORCH

A GUIDE TO DEEP LEARNING AND ARTIFICIAL INTELLIGENCE

Mark Bryan

Copyright

TABLE OF CONTENTS

CHAPTER 1: GETTING STARTED WITH PYTORCH

Welcome to the journey of mastering PyTorch, a dynamic and versatile open-source deep learning framework that has revolutionized the world of artificial intelligence. In the ever-evolving landscape of machine learning, PyTorch stands as a beacon of innovation and simplicity, empowering developers to unravel the complexities of deep learning with grace.

1. What PyTorch Really Is

At its core, PyTorch is a Python-based scientific computing package serving as a powerhouse for building and training neural networks. What sets PyTorch apart is its dynamic computational graph, enabling developers to define and modify models on the fly. This flexibility not only facilitates intuitive experimentation but also fosters a deep understanding of the intricate workings of neural networks.

2. A Brief History of PyTorch

To comprehend the significance of PyTorch, let's rewind to its inception. Developed by the Facebook AI Research lab (FAIR), PyTorch emerged in 2016 as an open-source project. Its origins lie in the quest for a framework that seamlessly blends flexibility with computational efficiency. Over the years, PyTorch has evolved in response to the needs of researchers and developers alike, earning its reputation as a go-to tool in the deep learning community.

3. Why PyTorch is Highly Recommended

PyTorch's ascent to prominence is not merely a coincidence; it's a testament to its user-centric design and robust capabilities. Its dynamic computational graph facilitates a natural expression of complex ideas, making it an ideal choice for both beginners and seasoned researchers. The framework's emphasis on simplicity accelerates the learning curve, enabling developers to focus on the intricacies of their models rather than wrestling with the framework itself.

Furthermore, PyTorch's active community and comprehensive documentation create an ecosystem that nurtures collaboration and continuous learning. The framework has become synonymous with cutting-edge research, often being the tool of choice for pushing the boundaries of what's possible in artificial intelligence.

As you embark on this exploration of PyTorch, prepare to unlock the full potential of deep learning and artificial intelligence. Whether you're a novice eager to grasp the fundamentals or an experienced developer seeking to elevate your skills, this guide is crafted to illuminate the path toward PyTorch mastery. Let the journey begin!

Welcome to the foundational chapter of your PyTorch journey, where we dive headfirst into the heart of this powerful framework. This chapter is designed to be your compass, guiding you through the initial steps of understanding PyTorch, from its basic principles to the hands-on application of fundamental concepts.

1.1 Understanding the Basics

Let's start at the beginning – understanding the fundamental building blocks of PyTorch.

Imagine PyTorch as your creative canvas, where you'll paint intricate neural networks and bring artificial intelligence to life. To embark on this artistic endeavor, we'll first explore the basics:

a. Tensors and Operations: At the core of PyTorch lies the concept of tensors, which are akin to mathematical arrays. Discover how to create tensors, manipulate their dimensions, and perform essential operations. This knowledge lays the groundwork for expressing data and computations within the PyTorch framework.

b. Variables and Gradients: Enter the realm of automatic differentiation. Learn about PyTorch Variables, entities that not only store tensors but also keep track of operations performed on them. Delve into the concept of gradients, where PyTorch's dynamic computation graph shines. Grasp how PyTorch automatically computes and handles gradients, a crucial aspect in training neural networks.

c. Navigating PyTorch Documentation: Unravel the treasure trove of PyTorch's documentation. A developer's best friend, the documentation is your guide to understanding functions, modules, and nuances within the framework. Learn effective ways to navigate this vast resource, ensuring you can harness the full potential of PyTorch in your projects.

In this section, we lay the groundwork for your PyTorch exploration. The basics are not merely stepping stones; they are the foundation upon which you'll construct sophisticated deep learning models. As you grasp these essentials, you'll gain the confidence to express your ideas in the language of PyTorch, setting the stage for the exciting journey that lies ahead. So, let's embark on this learning adventure and make the basics of PyTorch second nature to you.

1.2 Installing PyTorch

Now that you've laid the groundwork by understanding the basics of PyTorch, it's time to set up your workshop. In this section, we'll guide you through the process of installing PyTorch, ensuring you have a robust environment ready for your deep learning endeavors.

a. Choosing the Right Environment:

Before we embark on the installation journey, it's essential to select the right environment for your PyTorch projects. Whether you're using a local machine, a cloud-based service, or a specialized platform, we'll provide insights to help you make an informed decision based on your specific needs.

Choosing the right environment for your PyTorch projects involves considering various factors to ensure optimal development, execution, and scalability. Here are the criteria to guide you in making an informed decision:

1. Hardware Resources:

- *Local Machine (CPU/GPU):* If you have a robust GPU on your local machine, you can leverage it for faster model training. However, PyTorch also runs efficiently on CPUs, making it accessible to a broader audience.

- Cloud Services (e.g., AWS, Google Cloud, Azure): Cloud platforms provide scalable GPU resources. Consider the complexity and size of your projects when choosing cloud-based services, as they offer flexibility in terms of computational power.

2. Project Scale and Complexity:

- Small to Medium Projects: For simpler projects or when learning PyTorch, a local machine might suffice. CPU-only installations can handle small to medium-scale tasks.

- Large-Scale Projects: For complex models, extensive datasets, or parallel processing, GPU-enabled environments, either on a local machine or in the cloud, are preferable to expedite computations.

3. Budget Constraints:

- *Local Machine:* Utilizing your local machine for development is cost-effective. However, it might have limitations in terms of hardware capabilities compared to cloud-based solutions.

- Cloud Services: Cloud platforms offer pay-as-you-go models, but costs can escalate for resource-intensive tasks. Consider your budget constraints and choose a solution that aligns with your financial considerations.

4. Collaboration and Accessibility:

- *Local Machine:* Ideal for individual projects or small teams working in close proximity. Collaborating on a local machine may require additional setup for version control and sharing resources.

- *Cloud Services:* Facilitates collaboration in distributed teams. Cloud-based environments provide accessibility from anywhere, ensuring seamless collaboration and version control.

5. Resource Management and Isolation:

- *Virtual Environments:* Consider using virtual environments to isolate project dependencies. This ensures that different projects have distinct environments, preventing conflicts between package versions.

- *Containerization (e.g., Docker):* For consistent deployment across different environments, containerization allows you to encapsulate your application and its dependencies. Docker, for instance, provides a portable and reproducible environment.

6. Learning and Experimentation:

- *Local Machine:* Well-suited for learning and experimentation due to its simplicity and ease of setup.

- *Cloud Services:* Cloud platforms offer a playground for experimenting with different hardware configurations. Take advantage of cloud-based resources to test models in diverse environments.

By considering these criteria, you can tailor your PyTorch environment to meet the specific needs of your projects, ensuring efficiency, scalability, and a seamless development experience.

b. Installing PyTorch:

With your environment in place, let's dive into the step-by-step process of installing PyTorch. Whether you're a seasoned developer or a newcomer, we'll cater to your needs with clear instructions for various setups – be it CPU-only or GPU-enabled installations. Learn the commands, understand the dependencies, and troubleshoot common issues to ensure a smooth installation process.

Installing PyTorch involves several steps, and the process can vary based on your operating system and hardware configuration. Below, I'll provide a generic step-by-step guide for a CPU-only installation on a local machine using Python and pip. If you plan to use GPU acceleration or a different setup, you may need to consult the official PyTorch installation documentation for specific instructions.

Step-by-Step Guide to Installing PyTorch (CPU-only)

1. Prerequisites:

- Ensure you have Python installed on your system. You can download Python from [python.org](https://www.python.org/downloads/).

2. Create a Virtual Environment (Optional):

- It's good practice to work within a virtual environment to isolate your project dependencies. Use the following commands in your terminal or command prompt:

```bash
python -m venv myenv   # Replace 'myenv' with your preferred environment name

source myenv/bin/activate  # Activate the virtual environment (Linux/Mac)

# OR

.\myenv\Scripts\activate  # Activate the virtual environment (Windows)
```

3. Install PyTorch:

- With your virtual environment activated, use pip to install PyTorch. Visit the [official PyTorch website](https://pytorch.org/get-started/locally/)

to get the specific pip install command for your system. The he command for a CPU-only installation on a Linux/Mac system is:

```bash
pip install torch torchvision torchaudio
```

- On Windows, the command is:

```bash
pip install torch==1.10.0+cpu torchvision==0.11.1+cpu torchaudio==0.10.0+cpu -f https://download.pytorch.org/whl/cpu/torch_stable.html
```

```
` ` `
```

4. Verification:

- After installation, verify that PyTorch is installed correctly by opening a Python interpreter (type `python` in your terminal or command prompt) and running the following commands:

```python
` ` `python
import torch
print(torch.__version__)
` ` `
```

- This should print the installed PyTorch version without any errors.

5. Deactivate Virtual Environment (Optional):

- If you used a virtual environment, deactivate it when you're done working on your project:

```bash
deactivate  # Deactivate the virtual environment
```

Congratulations! You have successfully installed PyTorch on your local machine. Keep in mind that specific details might change based on updates or your system configuration, so always refer to the [official PyTorch installation documentation](https://pytorch.org/get-started/locally/) for the most accurate and up-to-date information.

c. Verifying Your Installation:

Installation is just the first step. We'll guide you through a series of checks to ensure that PyTorch is properly installed and configured. Verify your installation by running simple Python scripts, testing tensor operations, and confirming that your system is ready for the exciting journey of developing with PyTorch.

Verifying your PyTorch installation ensures that the framework is correctly set up on your system. Here are the steps to verify your PyTorch installation:

1. Open a Python Interpreter:

   - Open a terminal or command prompt on your system.

2. Start the Python Interpreter:

   - Type `python` or `python3` and press Enter to start the Python interpreter.

3. Import PyTorch:

- Once in the Python interpreter, import the PyTorch library by running the following command:

```python
import torch
```

4. Check PyTorch Version:

- After importing PyTorch, print the installed version using the following command:

```python
print(torch.__version__)
```

- This command should output the version number of the installed PyTorch.

5. Test a Simple Operation:

- Conduct a simple operation using PyTorch to ensure basic functionality. For example:

```python
x = torch.ones(5, 5)
y = x + 3
print(y)
```

- This creates a 5x5 tensor of ones, adds 3 to each element, and prints the resulting tensor.

6. Check for GPU Availability (Optional):

- If you have GPU support and have installed PyTorch with GPU capabilities, you can check if your system has a GPU available. Run the following command:

```python
print(torch.cuda.is_available())
```

- This command should return `True` if a GPU is available; otherwise, it will return `False`.

7. Exit the Python Interpreter:

- Type `exit()` or press `Ctrl + D` to exit the Python interpreter.

By following these steps, you can confirm that PyTorch is installed correctly, check the version, ensure basic functionality, and verify GPU availability if applicable. If any step encounters errors, double-check your installation process and refer to the [official PyTorch

documentation](https://pytorch.org/get-started/l
ocally/) for troubleshooting tips.

d. Virtual Environments and Best Practices:

Virtual Environments: A Developer's Oasis

In the vast landscape of software development,
the concept of virtual environments serves as a
crucial tool for maintaining order, managing
dependencies, and ensuring project
reproducibility. Let's dive into the essence of
virtual environments and why they are
considered a developer's oasis.

1. Isolation and Independence:

- *Problem:* Imagine having multiple projects with distinct sets of dependencies. Without virtual environments, managing these dependencies becomes a delicate balancing act, risking conflicts and version mismatches.

- *Solution:* Virtual environments provide isolated spaces for each project, shielding them from the chaos of conflicting dependencies. This isolation ensures that changes made in one environment do not affect others, fostering independence and modularity.

2. Dependency Management:

- **Problem:** Different projects may require different versions of libraries or packages.

Managing these dependencies globally can lead to conflicts and hinder the development process.

- **Solution:** With virtual environments, each project can have its own set of dependencies. This allows developers to specify and manage dependencies locally, ensuring that each project operates with its intended configurations.

3. Clean Development Environment:

- *Problem:* As projects progress, clutter accumulates in the form of installed packages, libraries, and configurations. A cluttered environment can lead to confusion and hinder reproducibility.

- **Solution:** Virtual environments offer a clean slate for each project. By encapsulating dependencies within the environment, developers create a pristine space where only the necessary components exist. This cleanliness enhances the reproducibility of the development environment.

4. Version Control and Collaboration:

- *Problem:* Collaboration becomes challenging when team members use different versions of libraries or tools. Version mismatches can lead to inconsistent results and hinder collaboration.

- *Solution:* Virtual environments can be version-controlled. By sharing the environment configuration file (e.g., `requirements.txt`), collaborators can synchronize their development environments, ensuring consistency and facilitating seamless collaboration.

5. Easy Setup and Reproducibility:

- *Problem:* Setting up a new development environment or reproducing an existing one can be time-consuming and error-prone.

- *Solution:* Virtual environments simplify this process. Developers can share environment configuration files, allowing others to recreate the exact environment effortlessly. This promotes reproducibility across different systems and stages of a project.

6. Python's `venv` Module:

- *Solution:* Python provides a built-in module called `venv` that allows developers to create virtual environments effortlessly. Using commands like `python -m venv myenv`, developers can set up a virtual environment named `myenv` and activate it with platform-specific commands (`source myenv/bin/activate` for Linux/Mac, `.\myenv\Scripts\activate` for Windows).

In essence, virtual environments offer developers a controlled and organized space to build and experiment with their projects. They promote good development practices, enhance collaboration, and ensure that the development journey remains a smooth and reproducible experience. Consider virtual environments as your oasis in the coding desert, providing a reliable and structured foundation for your projects to flourish.

Steps for Creating Virtual Environments for PyTorch Projects:

1. Open a Terminal or Command Prompt:

- Open a terminal or command prompt in the directory where you want to create your PyTorch project.

2. Use the `venv` Module to Create a Virtual Environment:

- Run the following command to create a virtual environment. Replace `myenv` with your chosen environment name.

```bash
python -m venv myenv   # Replace 'myenv' with your chosen environment name
```

3. Activate the Virtual Environment:

- Activate the virtual environment using platform-specific commands. Note that activation commands differ between operating systems.

- For Linux/Mac:

```bash
source myenv/bin/activate
```

- For Windows:

```bash
.\myenv\Scripts\activate
```

4. Verify the Activation:

- Confirm that you are in the virtual environment by checking if the environment name appears in your terminal prompt.

5. Install PyTorch in the Virtual Environment:

- While the virtual environment is active, you can use `pip` to install PyTorch. Visit the [official PyTorch website](https://pytorch.org/get-started/locally/) to get the specific pip install command for your system.

6. Install Other Project Dependencies (Optional):

- If your PyTorch project requires additional dependencies, install them using `pip` while the virtual environment is active.

```bash
pip install package_name
```

7. Deactivate the Virtual Environment:

- When you're finished working on your PyTorch project, deactivate the virtual environment.

```bash

deactivate

```

By following these steps, you can create a virtual environment tailored for your PyTorch project, providing a controlled and isolated space for managing dependencies specific to your deep learning endeavors.

Creating your first PyTorch program involves writing a simple script to familiarize yourself with basic PyTorch operations. Below are the steps for creating your first PyTorch program within the context of a virtual environment:

Steps for Your First PyTorch Program:

1. Activate Your Virtual Environment:

- Open a terminal or command prompt and navigate to the directory where your virtual environment is located.

- Activate the virtual environment:

- For Linux/Mac:

```bash
source myenv/bin/activate
```

- For Windows:

```bash
.\myenv\Scripts\activate
```

2. Create a New Python Script:

- Using a text editor or an integrated development environment (IDE) of your choice, create a new Python script. Let's name it `first_pytorch_program.py`.

3. Write Your First PyTorch Program:

- In your `first_pytorch_program.py` script, write a simple PyTorch program. Here's an example that creates a tensor and performs a basic operation:

```python
import torch

# Create a tensor
x = torch.tensor([[1, 2], [3, 4]])

# Print the tensor
print("Original Tensor:")
print(x)

# Perform a simple operation
y = x + 5

# Print the result
```

```
print("'\nTensor after Operation:")

print(y)

` ` `
```

- This program creates a 2x2 tensor, adds 5 to each element, and prints the original and modified tensors.

4. Save and Close the Script:

- Save your changes in the script and close the editor or IDE.

5. Run Your PyTorch Program:

- In the terminal or command prompt, make sure your virtual environment is still active.

- Run your PyTorch program:

```bash
python first_pytorch_program.py
```

- This command executes your script, and you should see the output of your PyTorch program in the terminal.

6. Deactivate the Virtual Environment:

- When you're done running your PyTorch program, deactivate the virtual environment:

```bash
deactivate
```

Congratulations! You've just created and executed your first PyTorch program. This simple script provides a foundational understanding of creating tensors and performing operations within the PyTorch framework. Feel free to explore more complex operations and gradually build your expertise in PyTorch.

"That's it for chapter one! I hope you're feeling excited and ready to take on the next chapter. Remember, practice makes perfect, so keep at it and don't be afraid to make mistakes. PyTorch is a powerful tool, and with the right mindset and dedication, you'll be able to master it in no time. Stay tuned for chapter two, where we will go deeper into PyTorch essentials. And remember, have fun and enjoy the journey!

CHAPTER 2: PYTORCH ESSENTIALS

Welcome to the heart of PyTorch Essentials! In this chapter, we delve into the very fabric that makes PyTorch an exceptional deep learning framework—tensors and operations. These foundational elements form the building blocks of your journey into the intricate world of neural networks and artificial intelligence.

2.1 Tensors and Operations: The Bedrock of PyTorch

Understanding Tensors: The Essence of PyTorch

Tensors are the fundamental data structures in PyTorch, analogous to arrays or matrices in traditional mathematics. They are the vessels that carry data through the intricate web of neural network computations. Let's explore the key aspects of tensors:

1. Creation and Initialization:

In the realm of PyTorch, the creation and initialization of tensors mark the inception of your journey into the world of data representation and manipulation. Tensors, akin to mathematical arrays, are the elemental entities that carry the weight of information within the PyTorch framework. Let's unravel the nuances of creating and initializing tensors, the very building blocks of your PyTorch odyssey.

1. Creation of Tensors: Crafting the Blueprint

When you embark on creating tensors in PyTorch, you are essentially crafting the blueprint for your data structures. Here are the key aspects to grasp:

Scalar Tensors:

Imagine a single data point, a solitary number in the vast landscape of data. In PyTorch, this is encapsulated in a scalar tensor.

```python
import torch

# Creating a scalar tensor
scalar_tensor = torch.tensor(42)
```

```
```

The `torch.tensor()` function serves as your artisan's brush, shaping the scalar tensor with the value `42`. This seemingly simple act sets the stage for more complex data structures.

Multi-dimensional Tensors:

As you traverse beyond the realm of single values, you'll find the need for multi-dimensional tensors. These tensors serve as containers for more intricate data, such as matrices.

```python
```

```
# Creating a 2x2 matrix tensor

matrix_tensor = torch.tensor([[1, 2], [3, 4]])

```
```

Here, the `matrix_tensor` takes form as a 2x2 matrix, capturing relationships and patterns within the data. The creation process unfolds with clarity, laying the groundwork for manipulating structured information.

Certainly! Let's dive into code examples and applications for creating and initializing tensors in PyTorch.

Applications:
```

1. Image Processing:

```python
import torch
import torchvision.transforms as transforms
from PIL import Image

# Load an image
image = Image.open("example_image.jpg")

# Convert the image to a PyTorch tensor
transform = transforms.ToTensor()
image_tensor = transform(image)
```

```python
# Perform operations on the image tensor (e.g.,
normalization)
normalized_image = (image_tensor - 0.5) / 0.5


# Display the original and normalized tensors
print("Original Image Tensor:")
print(image_tensor)


print("\nNormalized Image Tensor:")
print(normalized_image)
```


2. Neural Network Initialization:


```python
```

```python
import torch.nn as nn


# Define a simple neural network
class SimpleNet(nn.Module):
    def __init__(self):
        super(SimpleNet, self).__init__()
        self.fc = nn.Linear(10, 5)  # Fully connected
layer with input size 10 and output size 5


    def forward(self, x):
        return self.fc(x)


# Create an instance of the neural network
model = SimpleNet()
```

```python
# Print the initialized weights of the fully connected
layer
print("Initialized Weights:")
print(model.fc.weight)
```

3. Data Generation for Machine Learning:

```python
import torch
from sklearn.datasets import make_classification

# Generate a synthetic dataset using scikit-learn
```

```
X, y = make_classification(n_samples=100,

n_features=20, n_informative=10, n_classes=2,

random_state=42)


# Convert NumPy arrays to PyTorch tensors

X_tensor = torch.tensor(X, dtype=torch.float32)

y_tensor = torch.tensor(y, dtype=torch.float32)


# Print the shapes of the tensors

print("X Tensor Shape:", X_tensor.shape)

print("y Tensor Shape:", y_tensor.shape)
```
```

These examples showcase how creating and initializing tensors play a crucial role in various
```

applications, including image processing, neural network initialization, and data generation for machine learning tasks. The ability to seamlessly convert data into tensors and perform operations is a fundamental skill in PyTorch, enabling you to work with diverse datasets and build powerful deep learning models.

2 Initialization of Tensors: Breathing Life into Data

In the realm of PyTorch, the creation of tensors lays the foundation, but it is in their initialization that these tensors come to life.

The process of initialization is akin to breathing life into the structures you've crafted—assigning values, defining data types, and imbuing tensors with specific characteristics. This step is not merely technical; it is the act of giving purpose and meaning to the raw numerical containers. Let's delve into the nuances of tensor initialization and understand how it brings vitality to your data.

Default Initialization: The Canvas Awaits

When you create a tensor without explicitly specifying its values, PyTorch employs default initialization. This default initialization fills the tensor with values that depend on the current state of memory. While seemingly abstract, this method ensures that tensors are not born empty; they come with values ready to be molded by your data.

Example:

```python
import torch

# Default initialization of a tensor
default_initialized_tensor = torch.tensor([1.0, 2.0, 3.0])
```

```
# Printing the default-initialized tensor

print("Default Initialized Tensor:")

print(default_initialized_tensor)

```
```

Here, the tensor is born with values [1.0, 2.0, 3.0], ready to be part of a broader narrative.

Specifying Data Types: Precision in the Details

As you breathe life into tensors, specifying their data types becomes an expressive act. Data types define the precision with which numbers are stored and manipulated. This
```

precision is crucial for tasks where accuracy matters, such as scientific computations or machine learning.

Example:

```python
# Initializing a tensor with a specific data type
float_tensor = torch.tensor([1.0, 2.0, 3.0], dtype=torch.float32)

# Printing the tensor with specified data type
print("Float Tensor:")
print(float_tensor)
```

Here, the tensor is explicitly defined as a `float32` data type, showcasing meticulousness in representing real-world data.

Applications: Where Initialization Comes Alive

1. Image Processing:

- When processing images, tensor initialization is the gateway. Converting images into tensors allows for seamless integration into neural network architectures.

```python
```

```python
import torch

import torchvision.transforms as transforms

from PIL import Image


# Load an image

image = Image.open("example_image.jpg")


# Convert the image to a PyTorch tensor

transform = transforms.ToTensor()

image_tensor = transform(image)


# Perform operations on the image tensor (e.g.,
normalization)

normalized_image = (image_tensor - 0.5) / 0.5
```

```python
# Display the original and normalized tensors

print("Original Image Tensor:")

print(image_tensor)


print("\nNormalized Image Tensor:")

print(normalized_image)
```

2. Neural Network Initialization:

- In the context of neural networks, initializing weights and biases is a critical step. It sets the stage for effective learning during the training process.

```python
```

```python
import torch.nn as nn


# Define a simple neural network
class SimpleNet(nn.Module):
    def __init__(self):
        super(SimpleNet, self).__init__()
        self.fc = nn.Linear(10, 5)  # Fully connected
layer with input size 10 and output size 5


    def forward(self, x):
        return self.fc(x)


# Create an instance of the neural network
model = SimpleNet()
```

```
# Print the initialized weights of the fully
connected layer
print("Initialized Weights:")
print(model.fc.weight)
```

3. Data Generation for Machine Learning:

- Initializing tensors becomes instrumental when dealing with data generated for machine learning tasks. Converting datasets into tensors sets the stage for training models.

```python
import torch
from sklearn.datasets import make_classification
```

```
# Generate a synthetic dataset using scikit-learn
X, y = make_classification(n_samples=100,
n_features=20, n_informative=10, n_classes=2,
random_state=42)


# Convert NumPy arrays to PyTorch tensors
X_tensor = torch.tensor(X, dtype=torch.float32)
y_tensor = torch.tensor(y, dtype=torch.float32)


# Print the shapes of the tensors
print("X Tensor Shape:", X_tensor.shape)
print("y Tensor Shape:", y_tensor.shape)
```
```
```

In each of these applications, the act of initializing tensors breathes life into the data. It transforms numerical entities into meaningful representations—be it images, neural network weights, or datasets ready for the machine learning journey. The precision and expressiveness embedded in tensor initialization pave the way for accurate and purposeful computations in the diverse landscape of PyTorch applications. The canvas is yours, and with each initialized tensor, a narrative begins to unfold in the language of artificial intelligence.

Creating tensors is akin to shaping raw materials, but the process gains vitality through initialization. Let's breathe life into tensors by exploring initialization techniques:

The Significance:

The creation and initialization of tensors in PyTorch are not mere technicalities; they are the pivotal steps in sculpting a language for expressing complex data structures. From solitary values to intricate matrices, each tensor forged in this process is a vessel of potential insights. As you traverse the landscapes of neural networks and deep learning, your ability to create and initialize tensors becomes the bedrock upon which the intelligence of your models stands. Embrace the artistry of crafting tensors, for in their essence lies the ability to speak the language of artificial intelligence.

2. Tensor Properties: Unveiling the Essence of Data

Understanding the properties of tensors in PyTorch is akin to deciphering the language with which your data speaks. Tensors are not mere numerical containers; they possess inherent characteristics that provide insights into their structure, dimensions, and nature.

Let's delve into the properties of tensors, unraveling the essence of these foundational data structures.

1. Shape: The Blueprint of Tensors

The shape of a tensor is its defining characteristic, outlining the arrangement of elements along each dimension. It's like the blueprint of a building, specifying the structure and layout. In PyTorch, accessing the shape is fundamental to understanding the tensor's structure.

Example:

```python
import torch


# Creating a 2x3 matrix tensor

matrix_tensor = torch.tensor([[1, 2, 3], [4, 5, 6]])


# Accessing the shape of the tensor

tensor_shape = matrix_tensor.shape


# Printing the shape

print("Tensor Shape:", tensor_shape)
```

Here, the tensor shape is `(2, 3)`, signifying a 2x3 matrix.

2. Size: The Total Number of Elements

While shape gives you the arrangement, size provides the total count of elements within the tensor. It's akin to knowing the total floor area of a building.

Example:

```python
# Accessing the size of the tensor
tensor_size = matrix_tensor.size()
```

```
# Printing the size

print("Tensor Size:", tensor_size)

```
```

The tensor size here is `6`, indicating there are six elements in the 2x3 matrix.

3. Data Type: Precision in Representation

The data type of a tensor defines the precision with which numerical values are stored. It ensures consistency in computations and is crucial in scenarios where accuracy matters.
```

Example:

```python
# Accessing the data type of the tensor
tensor_data_type = matrix_tensor.dtype

# Printing the data type
print("Tensor Data Type:", tensor_data_type)
```

In this example, the tensor has a default data type (`torch.int64`), representing 64-bit integer values.

4. Device: Where the Tensor Resides

Tensors can reside either on a CPU or a GPU. Knowing the device on which a tensor resides is crucial for optimizing computations.

Example:

```python
# Moving the tensor to the GPU if available
gpu_tensor = matrix_tensor.to("cuda" if torch.cuda.is_available() else "cpu")

# Accessing the device of the tensor
tensor_device = gpu_tensor.device
```

```
# Printing the device

print("Tensor Device:", tensor_device)

` ` `
```

The tensor device here indicates whether it's on the CPU or GPU.

Applications: Where Tensor Properties Shine

1. Neural Network Architecture:

  - In deep learning, understanding the input and output shapes of tensors is pivotal in designing neural network architectures. Knowing the size of tensors flowing through layers is essential for proper connectivity.

2. Data Preprocessing:

- When working with diverse datasets, the shape and size of tensors play a crucial role in preprocessing steps. Reshaping and resizing tensors are common operations in data preparation.

3. Performance Optimization:

- The data type and device properties of tensors are crucial for performance optimization. Employing lower-precision data types and utilizing GPU acceleration can significantly speed up computations.

The Significance: Decoding the Language of Tensors

The properties of tensors in PyTorch are not mere technical details; they are the vocabulary with which you communicate with your data. The shape, size, data type, and device properties collectively form a language that encapsulates the essence of information. In every application—be it deep learning, scientific computing, or data analysis—understanding and leveraging these tensor properties is akin to deciphering the unique language spoken by your data. With each property, a story unfolds, and the narrative of your PyTorch journey gains clarity and precision.

3. Operations on Tensors:Unleashing Computational Power

Tensors, the fundamental data structures in PyTorch, come alive through operations, offering a rich toolkit for numerical computations. From basic arithmetic to advanced manipulations, tensor operations form the backbone of various applications.

Let's embark on a journey through the landscape of tensor operations, exploring their versatility and applications.

1. Basic Arithmetic Operations: The Foundation

At the core of tensor operations lie elementary arithmetic functions—addition, subtraction, multiplication, and division. These operations empower you to perform element-wise manipulations on tensors, forming the building blocks for more complex computations.

Example:

```python
import torch


# Creating two tensors
tensor_a = torch.tensor([[1, 2], [3, 4]])
tensor_b = torch.tensor([[5, 6], [7, 8]])


# Addition
result_addition = tensor_a + tensor_b


# Subtraction
result_subtraction = tensor_a - tensor_b
```

```
# Multiplication

result_multiplication = tensor_a * tensor_b


# Division

result_division = tensor_a / tensor_b

` ` `
```

In this example, `result_addition`, `result_subtraction`, `result_multiplication`, and `result_division` showcase the versatility of basic arithmetic operations.

2. Mathematical Functions: Elevating Transformations

PyTorch provides a diverse set of mathematical functions that extend the capabilities of tensor operations. Trigonometric functions, exponential transformations, and more open doors to intricate computations.

Example:

```python
# Applying mathematical functions
import torch
import torch.nn.functional as F

# Creating a tensor
tensor_x = torch.tensor([1.0, 2.0, 3.0])
```

```
# Square root

result_sqrt = torch.sqrt(tensor_x)


# Sine function

result_sin = torch.sin(tensor_x)


# Softmax function (from torch.nn.functional)

result_softmax = F.softmax(tensor_x, dim=0)
```

Here, `result_sqrt`, `result_sin`, and `result_softmax` demonstrate the application of mathematical functions, expanding the transformative potential of tensor operations.

3. Advanced Operations: Mastery Unleashed

Beyond the basics, PyTorch supports advanced operations such as matrix multiplication, reshaping, and indexing. These operations are instrumental in complex tasks, particularly in the realm of deep learning.

Example:

```python
# Advanced tensor operations
import torch
```

```python
# Creating tensors

tensor_c = torch.tensor([[1, 2, 3], [4, 5, 6]])

tensor_d = torch.tensor([[7, 8], [9, 10], [11, 12]])


# Matrix multiplication

result_matmul = torch.mm(tensor_c, tensor_d)


# Reshaping

result_reshaped = tensor_c.view(-1)  # Flattening the tensor


# Indexing

element_at_index_2 = tensor_c[1, 2]
```
```
```

In this example, `result_matmul`, `result_reshaped`, and `element_at_index_2` showcase the prowess of advanced tensor operations.

Applications: A Tapestry of Utility

1. Neural Network Training:

- Tensor operations are the backbone of deep learning, facilitating the training of neural networks through operations like matrix multiplications and activation functions.

2. Data Analysis and Manipulation:

- In data science, tensor operations are indispensable for exploring and manipulating datasets, enabling tasks ranging from basic statistics to complex transformations.

3. Scientific Computing:

- Scientists leverage tensor operations for simulations and computations in various disciplines, relying on operations like element-wise arithmetic for numerical simulations.

The Essence: A Language of Computation

In the landscape of PyTorch, tensor operations speak a language of computation. They empower you to express complex transformations, unravel the intricacies within your data, and unleash computational power across diverse applications. With each operation, you shape the narrative of your computational journey, traversing a landscape where numerical precision meets transformative potential.

Beyond the Basics: Advanced Tensor Operations

As your understanding of tensors deepens, venture into more advanced operations that PyTorch offers:

1. Broadcasting: Seamless Harmony in Tensor Operations

Broadcasting is a remarkable feature in PyTorch that enhances the flexibility of tensor operations, enabling effortless computations on tensors with different shapes. This mechanism simplifies the need for explicit reshaping, making element-wise operations more intuitive and concise. Let's delve into the intricacies of broadcasting, exploring its principles, advantages, and practical applications.

Understanding Broadcasting: A Symphony of Dimensions

At its core, broadcasting allows PyTorch to perform operations on tensors with different shapes by implicitly expanding the smaller tensor to match the shape of the larger one. This expansion occurs in a way that aligns dimensions, facilitating seamless element-wise operations.

Example:

```python
import torch

# Creating a tensor
tensor_a = torch.tensor([[1, 2, 3], [4, 5, 6]])

# Broadcasting a scalar
result_broadcast_scalar = tensor_a + 2
```

Here, the scalar `2` is broadcasted to match the shape of `tensor_a`, enabling addition to each element effortlessly.

Broadcasting Rules: Dimensions in Harmony

To comprehend broadcasting, consider the following rules:

1. Mismatched Dimensions:

- If tensors have different dimensions, pad the smaller tensor's shape with ones on its left side until both shapes have the same length.

2. Differing Sizes in Dimensions:

- For each dimension where sizes differ, if one of them is 1, expand it along that dimension to match the size of the other.

These rules ensure that tensors of varying shapes can be seamlessly aligned for element-wise operations.

Example:

```python
# Broadcasting with two tensors
tensor_b = torch.tensor([10, 20, 30])
```

result_broadcasting = tensor_a + tensor_b

```
```

In this scenario, `tensor_b` is broadcasted to the shape of `tensor_a`, facilitating element-wise addition without explicit resizing.

Applications: Streamlining Computational Tasks

1. Efficient Batch Operations:

- Broadcasting streamlines batch operations in deep learning, enhancing code simplicity and computational efficiency.

```python
```

```
# Broadcasting in batch operations

import torch


# Creating a batch of matrices

batch_matrix = torch.rand((3, 1, 4, 4))

scalar_multiplier = 2.0


# Broadcasting the scalar to the batch

result_batch_operation    =    batch_matrix    *
scalar_multiplier
```
```

### 2. Simplified Image Processing:

  - Broadcasting proves useful in image processing tasks, simplifying operations on
```

entire images or image channels without explicit reshaping.

```python
# Broadcasting in image processing
import torch
import torchvision.transforms as transforms
from PIL import Image

# Load an image
image = Image.open("example_image.jpg")

# Convert the image to a PyTorch tensor
transform = transforms.ToTensor()
image_tensor = transform(image)
```

```
# Broadcasting to adjust image brightness

result_brightened_image = image_tensor + 0.2

` ` `
```

Benefits: Conciseness and Readability

The primary advantages of broadcasting lie in its ability to create concise and readable code. By eliminating the need for explicit reshaping or loops, broadcasting simplifies tensor operations, making code more intuitive and expressive.

Common Pitfalls: Grasping Broadcasting Rules

While broadcasting is a powerful tool, understanding the rules is crucial to avoid pitfalls. Ensuring a solid grasp of how PyTorch aligns dimensions during operations ensures correct and predictable results.

Broadcasting in PyTorch orchestrates an elegant harmony in tensor operations, enabling effortless computations on tensors with varying shapes. This feature is a key element in writing streamlined and readable code, particularly in domains like deep learning and numerical computing. Embracing broadcasting empowers you with a versatile tool that expands the possibilities of what can be achieved with tensor operations in PyTorch.

2. In-Place Operations:

In-Place Operations in PyTorch: Navigating the Fine Line of Mutability

In-place operations in PyTorch refer to operations that modify the content of a tensor without creating a new copy. Unlike standard operations that create a new tensor with the result, in-place operations directly modify the existing tensor. This concept introduces efficiency gains but also demands caution due to its impact on mutability. Let's delve into the world of in-place operations, understanding their mechanics, benefits, and potential pitfalls.

Understanding In-Place Operations: The Mutable Transformations

In-place operations directly alter the content of a tensor, making changes to the existing memory location rather than creating a new tensor. These operations are denoted by an underscore suffix in PyTorch function names (e.g., `add_`, `mul_`, `clamp_`).

Example:

```python
import torch

# Creating a tensor
tensor_a = torch.tensor([1, 2, 3])

# In-place addition
tensor_a.add_(2)

# The original tensor_a is modified
print("Modified Tensor:", tensor_a)
```

Here, `add_` is an in-place operation, directly modifying `tensor_a` by adding 2 to each element.

Benefits of In-Place Operations: Efficiency and Memory

1. Efficiency:
-In-place operations are more memory-efficient as they avoid creating additional tensors. This can be crucial when working with large datasets or models.

2. Reduced Memory Footprint:

- Since in-place operations modify the existing tensor, they result in a reduced memory footprint compared to creating new tensors.

Potential Pitfalls: Caution in Mutability

1. Unexpected Side Effects:

- In-place operations directly modify the original tensor, potentially leading to unexpected side effects, especially when reusing variables.

```python
# Potential side effect
tensor_b = tensor_a
```

```
tensor_a.add_(2)

print("Modified Tensor B:", tensor_b)

` ` `
```

In this example, modifying `tensor_a` has a side effect on `tensor_b`.

2. Difficulty in Debugging:

- In-place operations can make code harder to debug due to their mutability. Understanding when and where a tensor is modified becomes crucial for maintaining code integrity.

Best Practices: When to Use In-Place Operations

1. Performance Optimization:

- In-place operations are valuable in scenarios where memory efficiency and performance optimization are critical, such as deep learning training loops.

```python
# In-place operations in a training loop
for epoch in range(num_epochs):
    # Forward pass
    predictions = model(input_data)

    # Compute loss
    loss = compute_loss(predictions, target)
```

```
# Backward pass and optimization

optimizer.zero_grad()

loss.backward()

optimizer.step()

```
```

2. When Memory Constraints Matter:

- In applications with limited memory, such as edge devices or embedded systems, in-place operations can be beneficial in managing memory resources.

In-Place Operations and Immutability: Striking a Balance
```

While in-place operations offer efficiency gains, striking a balance between performance optimization and code maintainability is crucial. Adopting a cautious approach, especially in shared or collaborative codebases, ensures that mutability does not compromise code reliability.

3. Tensor Concatenation: Weaving Data Together

Tensor concatenation is a fundamental operation in PyTorch that involves combining multiple tensors along specified dimensions to create a larger tensor. This operation is akin to stitching together pieces of fabric to form a cohesive whole. Understanding tensor concatenation is essential for manipulating and structuring data efficiently. Let's explore the mechanics, applications, and nuances of tensor concatenation.

Understanding Tensor Concatenation: Stitching Data Seamlessly

Tensor concatenation in PyTorch is the process of joining tensors along a specified dimension. It allows you to combine tensors horizontally or vertically, depending on the application.

Example:

```python
import torch

# Creating two tensors
tensor_a = torch.tensor([[1, 2], [3, 4]])
tensor_b = torch.tensor([[5, 6]])

# Concatenating along dimension 0 (vertical concatenation)
result_vertical_concatenation = torch.cat((tensor_a, tensor_b), dim=0)
```

In this example,

`result_vertical_concatenation` is formed by

vertically concatenating `tensor_a` and `tensor_b` along dimension 0.

Concatenation along Dimensions: Vertical and Horizontal

1. Vertical Concatenation (`dim=0`):

- Vertically stacking tensors along rows, combining them into a larger tensor.

```python
# Vertical concatenation
result_vertical_concatenation = torch.cat((tensor_a, tensor_b), dim=0)
```

2. Horizontal Concatenation (`dim=1`):

- Horizontally concatenating tensors along columns, extending the width of the tensor.

```python
# Horizontal concatenation
tensor_c = torch.tensor([[7], [8]])
result_horizontal_concatenation =
torch.cat((tensor_a, tensor_c), dim=1)
```

Applications: Structuring Data

1. Dataset Creation:

- Concatenating tensors is common when creating datasets. For instance, combining images horizontally to form a dataset for image classification.

```python
# Concatenating image tensors horizontally
image_tensor1 = load_image("image1.jpg")
image_tensor2 = load_image("image2.jpg")


dataset = torch.cat((image_tensor1, image_tensor2), dim=1)
```

2. Sequence Data:

- Concatenating sequences along time steps when working with sequence-to-sequence models.

```python
# Concatenating sequences along time steps
sequence_timestep1 = torch.tensor([1, 2, 3])
sequence_timestep2 = torch.tensor([4, 5, 6])


combined_sequence =
torch.cat((sequence_timestep1, sequence_timestep2),
dim=0)
```

Concatenation Strategies: Static and Dynamic

1. Static Concatenation:

   - When the size of tensors is known beforehand, static concatenation using `torch.cat` is suitable.

```python
# Static concatenation
result_static_concatenation = torch.cat((tensor_a, tensor_b), dim=0)
```

2. Dynamic Concatenation:

- For dynamic scenarios where the size is not known in advance, using functions like `torch.stack` or `torch.cat` with dynamically generated tensors is preferable.

```python
# Dynamic concatenation using torch.stack
tensor_list = [tensor_a, tensor_b]
result_dynamic_concatenation = torch.stack(tensor_list, dim=0)
```

Concatenation Pitfalls: Dimension Mismatch

1. Dimension Mismatch:

- Ensure that tensors being concatenated have matching dimensions along the specified concatenation dimension. Dimension mismatches will result in errors.

```python
# Dimension mismatch example
tensor_c = torch.tensor([[7]])
result_invalid_concatenation = torch.cat((tensor_a, tensor_c), dim=0)  # Error: Dimensions do not match
```

Tensor concatenation in PyTorch is akin to weaving a tapestry of data, combining individual threads to create a cohesive whole.

Understanding how to concatenate tensors along different dimensions empowers you to structure and manipulate data efficiently, whether in the context of deep learning datasets, sequence models, or other applications. By mastering tensor concatenation, you gain a foundational skill for seamlessly handling and organizing diverse datasets in your PyTorch projects.

Why Tensors and Operations Matter in PyTorch:

1. Expressiveness:

- Tensors in PyTorch offer an expressive way to represent and manipulate data. The ease of creating tensors facilitates a seamless translation of mathematical concepts into practical code.

2. Flexibility:

- The versatility of tensor operations allows you to perform a wide range of computations efficiently. Whether you're adding constants, applying activation functions, or conducting complex matrix manipulations, PyTorch has you covered.

3. Integration with Neural Networks:

- Tensors are the backbone of neural networks. As you progress in your PyTorch journey, the operations you perform on tensors will become the very operations that drive the learning process within your neural networks.

2.2 Variables and Gradients: Unraveling the Dynamics of Differentiation

In PyTorch, Variables serve as dynamic and versatile entities that go beyond traditional tensors, playing a central role in facilitating automatic differentiation and forming the backbone of the autograd system. Understanding Variables is crucial for effectively harnessing the power of PyTorch in the realm of deep learning.

Creating Variables: The Genesis of Dynamism

Variables are instantiated by wrapping a PyTorch tensor, providing an enhanced container that not only holds data but also enables the tracking of operations for automatic differentiation. The `requires_grad` parameter indicates whether gradients should be tracked for the Variable.

```python
import torch
from torch.autograd import Variable

# Creating a Variable
x = Variable(torch.tensor([2.0]), requires_grad=True)
```

Here, `x` is a Variable initialized with a tensor of value 2.0, and `requires_grad=True` signals that gradients should be tracked for this Variable.

Creating a `Variable` in PyTorch involves a few essential steps. Below are the steps to create a `Variable`:

1. Import Necessary Libraries:

  - Import the required libraries, including the PyTorch library and the `Variable` class from the `torch.autograd` module.

```python
import torch
from torch.autograd import Variable
```

2. Create a PyTorch Tensor:

- Initialize a PyTorch tensor with the desired data.

```python
data = torch.tensor([2.0])
```

3. *Wrap the Tensor with a Variable:*

- Wrap the tensor with a `Variable` to create a dynamic entity capable of tracking operations for automatic differentiation. Use the `requires_grad` parameter to specify whether gradients should be tracked.

```python
```

```
x = Variable(data, requires_grad=True)

` ` `
```

Here, `x` is now a `Variable` that holds the tensor `data` and is set to track gradients during operations.

4. Perform Operations on the Variable (Optional):

- Optionally, you can perform mathematical operations on the created `Variable`. This step is crucial if you want to build a dynamic computational graph for subsequent gradient computation.

```python
```

$y = x2 + 3^*x + 1$

` ` `

Operations on the `Variable` contribute to the formation of a computational graph.

5. Visualize the Computational Graph (Optional):

- If needed, visualize the computational graph using tools like `torchviz` to gain insights into the flow of operations and dependencies.

```python
# Installing torchviz (if not installed)
# pip install torchviz
```

```
from torchviz import make_dot

# Creating a simple graph
make_dot(y, params={"x": x})
```
```
```

Visualization is optional but can be helpful for understanding complex models.

The above steps provide a general guideline for creating a `Variable` in PyTorch. Remember that PyTorch's dynamic computational graph and autograd system rely on the usage of `Variable` objects to enable automatic differentiation during model training.

Operations on Variables: Building a Dynamic Computational Graph

Variables shine when it comes to performing operations. Each operation on a Variable contributes to building a dynamic computational graph. This graph captures the dependencies between Variables, forming the basis for efficient computation of gradients during backpropagation.

```python
# Performing operations on a Variable
y = x2 + 3*x + 1
```

` ` `

In this example, the operations on Variable `x`—raising it to the power of 2, multiplying by 3, and adding 1—contribute to the formation of a computational graph.

Dynamic Computational Graph: Adapting to Data Changes

One of the distinctive features of Variables is their dynamic nature. Unlike static computational graphs, Variables allow for flexibility in defining and modifying models, especially in scenarios with varying input sizes. The autograd system dynamically constructs the graph based on the operations performed on Variables.

```python
# Dynamic computational graph
input_size = 5
weights = Variable(torch.randn(input_size, 1), requires_grad=True)
bias = Variable(torch.randn(1), requires_grad=True)

# Forward pass
output = torch.matmul(input_data, weights) + bias
```

```
# Backward pass
output.backward()
```

Here, the computational graph adapts to the changing input size, showcasing the flexibility of Variables.

Visualizing the Computational Graph: Insights through Visualization

Understanding the computational graph can be facilitated by tools like `torchviz`, which allows for the creation of graph visualizations. Visual representations provide insights into the flow of operations and dependencies.

```python
# Installing torchviz
# pip install torchviz


# Visualizing the graph
from torchviz import make_dot


# Creating a simple graph
y = x2 + 3*x + 1


# Visualizing the graph
make_dot(y, params={"x": x})
```

```
```

Visualizations generated by `torchviz` offer a clear representation of how operations on Variables contribute to the overall computational flow.

Applications: The Versatility of Variables in Deep Learning

1. Training Neural Networks:

- Variables form the basis for defining model parameters, and their dynamic nature facilitates the training of neural networks through the autograd system.

2. Custom Loss Functions:

- The flexibility of Variables allows for the creation of custom loss functions tailored to specific machine learning tasks.

Best Practices: Navigating the Variable Landscape

1. Understanding the Computational Graph:

- Visualization and comprehension of the computational graph contribute to effective debugging and optimization of models.

2. Memory Management:

- Clearing gradients using `zero_grad()` is essential to prevent memory leaks and ensure accurate gradient computation.

```python
# Clearing gradients
model.zero_grad()
```

Gradients in PyTorch: Guiding the Optimization Odyssey

Gradients in PyTorch represent the derivatives of a tensor with respect to some quantity, most commonly a scalar loss function. They play a pivotal role in the optimization process, guiding the adjustment of model parameters during training. Understanding gradients is essential for unraveling the magic behind automatic differentiation and the backpropagation algorithm in PyTorch.

Computing Gradients: The Essence of Backpropagation

The computation of gradients is initiated by invoking the `backward()` method on a tensor representing the scalar loss. This method traces back through the computational graph, computing the gradients of the loss with respect to each leaf tensor marked for gradient tracking.

```python
# Forward pass
loss = some_loss_function(output, target)

# Backward pass to compute gradients
loss.backward()
```

In this example, calling `loss.backward()` triggers the computation of gradients, allowing

PyTorch to populate the `grad` attributes of the tensors involved in the computation.

Accessing Gradients: Deriving Insights from Adjustments

Once gradients are computed, they can be accessed through the `grad` attribute of the tensors for which gradients were tracked during the backward pass.

```python
# Accessing gradients
gradient = x.grad
```

Here, `x.grad` contains the gradient of some quantity (usually the loss) with respect to the tensor `x`. Gradients provide information about how the output of the model or a function would change concerning changes in the input variables.

Dynamic Computational Graph: Gradients in the Autograd Flow

Gradients come to life within the dynamic computational graph constructed by PyTorch's autograd system. This dynamic nature allows for adaptability to varying model architectures and input sizes, making PyTorch well-suited for a variety of deep learning tasks.

```python
# Dynamic computational graph
input_size = 5
weights = Variable(torch.randn(input_size, 1),
requires_grad=True)
bias = Variable(torch.randn(1), requires_grad=True)

# Forward pass
output = torch.matmul(input_data, weights) + bias

# Backward pass to compute gradients
output.backward()
```

```
` ` `
```

In this scenario, the autograd system dynamically computes gradients during the backward pass, reflecting the impact of each operation on the model parameters.

Applications: Gradients in Model Optimization

1. Optimizing Model Parameters:

- Gradients guide the optimization process by indicating the direction and magnitude of adjustments needed for model parameters during training.

2. Backpropagation in Neural Networks:

- Gradients form the backbone of the backpropagation algorithm, allowing the efficient computation of parameter updates across layers in neural networks.

Best Practices: Navigating the Gradient Landscape

1. Gradient Clipping:

- To prevent exploding gradients, especially in deep networks, gradient clipping can be applied to limit the magnitude of gradients during training.

```python
# Gradient clipping example

torch.nn.utils.clip_grad_norm_(model.parameters(),
max_norm=1.0)
```

2. Zeroing Gradients:

- Clearing gradients using `zero_grad()` before each iteration is essential to prevent accumulation from previous batches.

```python
# Clearing gradients
model.zero_grad()
```

```
` ` `
```

Gradients in PyTorch serve as a compass, guiding the optimization journey of models through the vast landscape of parameter space. By understanding and leveraging gradients, practitioners can optimize model performance, foster faster convergence, and unravel the full potential of their PyTorch-powered models in the fascinating realm of machine learning.

Navigating PyTorch Documentation: A Compass for Seamless Exploration

Navigating PyTorch documentation is akin to having a robust compass in the vast terrain of deep learning. It's a skill that empowers developers and researchers to harness the full potential of PyTorch, unleashing the capabilities of this powerful framework. In this exploration, we'll delve into the essentials of navigating PyTorch documentation, providing you with a comprehensive guide for a seamless journey.

1. Understanding the Documentation Structure: Foundations of Exploration

The PyTorch documentation is well-organized, consisting of several sections that cater to different aspects of the framework. Key sections include:

- *Tutorials:* Practical guides to help you get started and master specific tasks.

- *Learn:* In-depth educational resources, including video lectures and courses.

- *API Documentation:* A detailed reference for PyTorch classes and functions.

- *Community and Resources:* Links to forums, community discussions, and additional learning materials.

2. Getting Started: Navigating the Tutorials

The "Tutorials" section is your gateway to hands-on learning. Start here to grasp the basics, understand key concepts, and build a strong foundation. Tutorials cover diverse topics, from basic tensor operations to advanced model training techniques. Whether you're a beginner or an experienced practitioner, these guides cater to different skill levels.

3. In-Depth Learning: Exploring the "Learn" Section

The "Learn" section provides a treasure trove of educational resources. Dive into video lectures, courses, and curated learning paths to deepen your understanding. From fundamental concepts to advanced topics, this section equips you with the knowledge needed to tackle complex challenges in the world of deep learning.

4. Reference Guide: Mastering the API Documentation

The API documentation is your go-to resource for understanding PyTorch classes, functions, and modules. Here, you'll find detailed descriptions, usage examples, and information about parameters and return values. The API documentation is crucial for integrating PyTorch into your projects, ensuring a solid understanding of the tools at your disposal.

5. Interactive Exploration: Using the Interactive Playground

The PyTorch website includes an interactive playground that allows you to experiment with PyTorch code directly in the browser. This hands-on approach is invaluable for testing ideas, understanding syntax, and gaining practical experience without setting up a local environment.

6. Community Engagement: Connecting with Peers

The "Community and Resources" section opens the door to a vibrant community of PyTorch enthusiasts. Engage in discussions, seek help on forums, and stay updated on the latest developments. The PyTorch community is a valuable asset for learning, sharing insights, and overcoming challenges.

7. Staying Updated: Exploring Release Notes and Announcements

Keep an eye on the "Release Notes" and announcements to stay updated on the latest features, improvements, and bug fixes. Understanding the evolution of PyTorch ensures you leverage the most recent advancements in your projects.

8. Contributing to PyTorch: Joining the Ecosystem

For those eager to contribute to PyTorch, the documentation provides guidelines on how to get involved. Whether it's fixing a bug, improving documentation, or adding new features, contributing to the PyTorch ecosystem is a rewarding way to give back to the community.

Navigating PyTorch documentation is not just a task; it's a skill that transforms you into a proficient explorer in the realm of deep learning. From tutorials to API documentation and community engagement, each section is a pathway to mastery. Embrace the documentation as your North Star, guiding you through the exciting and ever-expanding landscape of PyTorch.

Part 11: Deep Learning Foundations

CHAPTER 3:
FUNDAMENTALS OF
NEURAL NETWORKS

Welcome to the gateway of understanding the fundamentals of neural networks! In this chapter, we embark on a journey through the intricate terrain of the "Anatomy of a Neural Network." Let's unravel the core components that constitute the essence of these intelligent entities, breaking down complexities into digestible insights.

3.1 Anatomy of a Neural Network: Demystifying the Core Components

Neural networks, inspired by the human brain, possess a fascinating anatomy that powers their ability to learn and make predictions. In this section, we'll explore the fundamental elements that define the structure and functionality of a neural network.

1. Neurons: The Foundation of Intelligence

At the heart of every neural network are neurons, the building blocks of intelligence. These computational units process and transmit information, mimicking the neurons in the human brain. Neurons receive input, apply mathematical operations, and produce output, forming the bedrock of the network's computational power.

2. Layers: Crafting Hierarchical Representations

Neurons are organized into layers, creating a hierarchical structure within the neural network. This organization comprises three main types of layers:

- *Input Layer:* The entry point for data, where neurons receive initial signals.

- *Hidden Layers:* Intermediate layers responsible for feature extraction and abstraction.

- *Output Layer:* The final layer producing predictions or classifications based on processed information.

The arrangement and size of these layers define the network's architecture and its capacity to learn complex patterns.

3. Weights and Biases: Tuning the Learning Process

Connections between neurons are governed by weights and biases. Weights determine the strength of connections, while biases add flexibility. During training, these parameters are adjusted to minimize the difference between predicted and actual outputs. This fine-tuning process, known as backpropagation, is instrumental in enhancing the network's predictive capabilities.

4. Activation Functions: Injecting Non-Linearity

Activation functions introduce non-linearity, enabling neural networks to capture complex relationships within data. Common activation functions include ReLU, Sigmoid, and TanH. These functions contribute to the network's ability to model intricate patterns and dependencies.

5. Loss Function: Quantifying Prediction Accuracy

The loss function measures the disparity between predicted and actual outputs. During training, the goal is to minimize this loss, guiding the network toward more accurate predictions. Different tasks, such as classification or regression, require specific loss functions tailored to the nature of the problem.

6. Optimization Algorithms: Navigating the Learning Landscape

Optimization algorithms, like stochastic gradient descent (SGD) or Adam, guide the learning process by updating weights and biases based on computed gradients. These algorithms ensure that the neural network converges to an optimal state, minimizing the loss function and improving overall performance.

7. Backpropagation: The Engine of Learning

Backpropagation, the engine of learning in neural networks, involves computing gradients of the loss with respect to weights and biases. These gradients signal the network on how to adjust its parameters to enhance predictions. Backpropagation is a fundamental process driving the iterative refinement of the network's understanding.

8. Architectures: From Feedforward to Specialized Networks

Neural networks come in various architectures, each designed for specific tasks:

- *Feedforward Neural Networks (FNN):* Basic architecture with unidirectional information flow.

-*Convolutional Neural Networks (CNN):* Specialized for image-related tasks, leveraging convolutional layers.

- *Recurrent Neural Networks (RNN):* Suited for sequence data, incorporating feedback loops.

The choice of architecture depends on the nature of the data and the problem at hand.

The fundamentals of neural networks orchestrate a symphony of interconnected components, working in harmony to extract patterns, make predictions, and perform complex tasks. Understanding the anatomy of a neural network empowers practitioners to wield the power of intelligent models, transforming data into actionable insights. As we delve into the intricacies of neural networks, remember that each component contributes to the network's prowess, propelling us into the era of intelligent machines.

3.2 Activation Functions: Unveiling Non-Linearity

Activation functions are the secret sauce that introduces non-linearity into the behavior of neural networks, allowing them to model complex relationships and capture intricate patterns within data.

1. Sigmoid Function: The Squeeze and Squash

The Sigmoid function is a classic choice for activation in the output layer of binary classification tasks. It transforms input values into a range between 0 and 1, effectively squashing large positive or negative inputs. Its smooth and differentiable nature facilitates gradient-based optimization during training.

Here's a code example of the Sigmoid function in Python using PyTorch, along with a brief explanation:

```python
import torch
import torch.nn.functional as F


# Input tensor
x = torch.tensor([1.0, 2.0, 3.0])
```

```
# Applying Sigmoid activation
sigmoid_output = F.sigmoid(x)


# Print the result
print("Input tensor:", x)
print("Sigmoid output:", sigmoid_output)
```
```

**1. Import Libraries:** We import the necessary libraries, including PyTorch and its functional module (`torch.nn.functional`).

**2. Create Input Tensor:** We create a simple input tensor `x` with values `[1.0, 2.0, 3.0]`.
```

3. Apply Sigmoid Activation: The `F.sigmoid()` function is used to apply the Sigmoid activation to each element of the input tensor `x`. Sigmoid squashes input values into the range (0, 1), making it particularly useful for binary classification problems where you need to output probabilities.

4. Print Results: We print both the input tensor and the Sigmoid-transformed output.

Output:

```
```

Input tensor: tensor([1., 2., 3.])

Sigmoid output: tensor([0.7311, 0.8808, 0.9526])

` ` `

Explanation (continued):

- The Sigmoid function transformed the input values to a range between 0 and 1.
- Each element in the output tensor corresponds to the sigmoid activation of the respective element in the input tensor.
- The Sigmoid function is commonly used in the output layer of binary classification models to produce probabilities. For instance, in logistic regression, it's used to squash the raw

output into a probability of belonging to the positive class.

Feel free to experiment with different input values to see how the Sigmoid function behaves!

2. Hyperbolic Tangent (TanH): The Shifter and Squeezer

Similar to the Sigmoid function, TanH squashes input values, but in a range between -1 and 1. This centered output helps mitigate the vanishing gradient problem and is often used in hidden layers.

Here's a code example of the Hyperbolic Tangent (TanH) function in Python using PyTorch, along with a brief explanation:

```python
import torch
import torch.nn.functional as F

# Input tensor
x = torch.tensor([1.0, 2.0, 3.0])

# Applying TanH activation
tanh_output = F.tanh(x)
```

```
# Print the result

print("Input tensor:", x)

print("TanH output:", tanh_output)

` ` `
```

Explanation:

1. Import Libraries: We import the necessary libraries, including PyTorch and its functional module (`torch.nn.functional`).

2. Create Input Tensor: We create a simple input tensor `x` with values `[1.0, 2.0, 3.0]`.

3. Apply TanH Activation: The `F.tanh()` function is used to apply the TanH activation to each element of the input tensor `x`. TanH squashes input values into the range (-1, 1), shifting and squeezing them.

4. Print Results: We print both the input tensor and the TanH-transformed output.

Output:

```
` ` `
```

Input tensor: tensor([1., 2., 3.])

TanH output: tensor([0.7616, 0.9640, 0.9951])

```
` ` `
```

Explanation (continued):

- The TanH function transformed the input values to a range between -1 and 1.

- Each element in the output tensor corresponds to the TanH activation of the respective element in the input tensor.

- TanH is often used in hidden layers of neural networks to introduce non-linearity while avoiding the saturation issues that can occur with the Sigmoid function.

3. Rectified Linear Unit (ReLU): The Positive Activator

ReLU is a popular choice for hidden layers. It outputs the input directly if it is positive, and zero otherwise. This introduces sparsity and accelerates training, making it a go-to for many neural network architectures.

Here's a code example of the Rectified Linear Unit (ReLU) function in Python using PyTorch.

```python
import torch
import torch.nn.functional as F

# Input tensor
x = torch.tensor([-2.0, -1.0, 0.0, 1.0, 2.0])
```

```
# Applying ReLU activation

relu_output = F.relu(x)


# Print the result

print("Input tensor:", x)

print("ReLU output:", relu_output)

```
```

Explanation:

1. Import Libraries: We import the necessary libraries, including PyTorch and its functional module (`torch.nn.functional`).
```

2. Create Input Tensor: We create a simple input tensor `x` with values `[-2.0, -1.0, 0.0, 1.0, 2.0]`.

3. Apply ReLU Activation: The `F.relu()` function is used to apply the ReLU activation to each element of the input tensor `x`. ReLU sets negative values to zero and leaves positive values unchanged.

4. Print Results: We print both the input tensor and the ReLU-transformed output.

Output:

```
```

Input tensor: tensor([-2., -1., 0., 1., 2.])

ReLU output: tensor([0., 0., 0., 1., 2.])

```
` ` `
```

Explanation (continued):

- The ReLU function transforms the input values by setting negative values to zero.

- Each element in the output tensor corresponds to the ReLU activation of the respective element in the input tensor.

- ReLU is a popular choice for activation in hidden layers of neural networks because it introduces non-linearity and accelerates training by allowing only positive values to pass through.

4. Leaky ReLU: A Remedy for Dead Neurons

Leaky ReLU addresses the "dying ReLU" problem by allowing a small negative slope for negative inputs. This prevents neurons from becoming inactive during training.

Here's a code example:

```python
import torch
import torch.nn.functional as F
```

```
# Input tensor

x = torch.tensor([-2.0, -1.0, 0.0, 1.0, 2.0])


# Applying Leaky ReLU activation with a small
negative slope
leaky_relu_output        =        F.leaky_relu(x,
negative_slope=0.01)


# Print the result
print("Input tensor:", x)
print("Leaky ReLU output:", leaky_relu_output)
```
```

**Explanation:**
```

1. Import Libraries: We import the necessary libraries, including PyTorch and its functional module (`torch.nn.functional`).

2. Create Input Tensor: We create a simple input tensor `x` with values `[-2.0, -1.0, 0.0, 1.0, 2.0]`.

3. Apply Leaky ReLU Activation: The `F.leaky_relu()` function is used to apply the Leaky ReLU activation to each element of the input tensor `x`. Leaky ReLU allows a small negative slope for negative values, addressing the "dying ReLU" problem where some neurons become inactive during training.

4. *Print Results:* We print both the input tensor and the Leaky ReLU-transformed output.

Output:

```
` ` `

Input tensor: tensor([-2., -1.,  0.,  1.,  2.])
Leaky  ReLU  output:  tensor([-0.0200,  -0.0100,
0.0000,  1.0000,  2.0000])

` ` `
```

Explanation (continued):

- The Leaky ReLU function transforms the input values by allowing a small negative slope for negative values.

- Each element in the output tensor corresponds to the Leaky ReLU activation of the respective element in the input tensor.

- Leaky ReLU is designed to prevent neurons from becoming inactive during training, providing a remedy for the "dead neurons" issue associated with traditional ReLU.

5. Softmax: The Multiclass Maestro

Softmax is ideal for the output layer of multiclass classification tasks. It transforms input values into probabilities, ensuring that the sum of probabilities across all classes equals one.

Here's a code example along with a brief explanation:

```python
import torch
import torch.nn.functional as F


# Input tensor
x = torch.tensor([1.0, 2.0, 3.0])


# Applying Softmax activation
```

```
softmax_output = F.softmax(x, dim=0)


# Print the result

print("Input tensor:", x)

print("Softmax output:", softmax_output)
```
` ` `

Explanation:

1. Import Libraries: We import the necessary libraries, including PyTorch and its functional module (`torch.nn.functional`).

2. Create Input Tensor: We create a simple input tensor `x` with values `[1.0, 2.0, 3.0]`.

3. Apply Softmax Activation: The `F.softmax()` function is used to apply the Softmax activation to each element of the input tensor `x`. Softmax transforms input values into probabilities, ensuring that the sum of probabilities across all classes equals one.

4. Print Results: We print both the input tensor and the Softmax-transformed output.

Output:

```
```

Input tensor: tensor([1., 2., 3.])

Softmax output: tensor([0.0900, 0.2447, 0.6652])

```
```

Explanation (continued):

- The Softmax function transforms the input values into probabilities, making it suitable for the output layer of multiclass classification models.
- Each element in the output tensor corresponds to the probability of the respective class.
- Softmax ensures that the probabilities sum to one, providing a meaningful interpretation as class probabilities.

6. Swish: The Self-Gated Activation

Swish is a relatively recent addition that self-gates the input, potentially offering improved performance compared to traditional activations.

And of course, a code example of the Swish activation function in Python using PyTorch, along with a brief explanation:

```python
import torch
import torch.nn.functional as F
```

```python
# Input tensor
x = torch.tensor([1.0, 2.0, 3.0])

# Define the Swish activation function
def swish(x):
    return x * F.sigmoid(x)

# Applying Swish activation
swish_output = swish(x)

# Print the result
print("Input tensor:", x)
print("Swish output:", swish_output)
```
```
```

Explanation:

1. Import Libraries: We import the necessary libraries, including PyTorch and its functional module (`torch.nn.functional`).

2. Create Input Tensor: We create a simple input tensor `x` with values `[1.0, 2.0, 3.0]`.

3. Define Swish Activation Function: The `swish` function is defined as the product of the input `x` and the Sigmoid function of `x`.

4. Apply Swish Activation: We apply the Swish activation to each element of the input tensor `x`.

5. Print Results: We print both the input tensor and the Swish-transformed output.

Output:

```
` ` `

Input tensor: tensor([1., 2., 3.])
Swish output: tensor([0.7311, 1.8851, 2.9156])

` ` `
```

Explanation (continued):

- The Swish function is a self-gated activation that introduces a gating mechanism, potentially offering improved performance compared to traditional activations.

- Each element in the output tensor corresponds to the Swish activation of the respective element in the input tensor.

- Swish is designed to combine the linearity of the identity function with the non-linearity of the sigmoid function, aiming to capture complex patterns in the data.

7. Choosing the Right Activation: Art and Science

The selection of activation functions is both an art and a science. It depends on the specific characteristics of your data, the nature of the problem, and the architecture of your neural network. Experimentation and fine-tuning are key in finding the most suitable activation for your model.

Activation functions infuse neural networks with vitality, enabling them to learn and adapt to the complexities of data. Each function has its unique characteristics, influencing the learning dynamics of the network. As you explore the world of activation functions, remember that the choice you make plays a pivotal role in shaping the behavior of your neural network and unlocking its full potential.

3.3 Loss Functions: Unraveling the Essence

Loss functions, also known as objective functions or cost functions, serve as the compass guiding our neural networks during the training process. They quantify the disparity between predicted and actual outputs, providing a measure of how well our model is performing.

1. Mean Squared Error (MSE): The Pursuit of Precision

MSE is a widely-used loss function for regression tasks. It calculates the average squared difference between predicted and actual values. Minimizing MSE encourages the model to produce predictions closely aligned with the true values.

Here's a code example that demonstrates the calculation of Mean Squared Error (MSE) using PyTorch:

```python
import torch
import torch.nn.functional as F

# Example: Predicted values from the model
predictions = torch.tensor([2.0, 4.0, 6.0, 8.0])

# Example: True values (actual ground truth)
actual_values = torch.tensor([1.5, 4.5, 5.5, 8.5])

# Calculating Mean Squared Error (MSE)
mse_loss = F.mse_loss(predictions, actual_values)

# Print the result
print("Predicted values:", predictions)
```

```
print("True values:", actual_values)
print("Mean Squared Error (MSE):",
mse_loss.item())
```

Explanation:

1. Import Libraries: We import the necessary libraries, including PyTorch and its functional module (`torch.nn.functional`).

2. Example Data: We define two tensors, `predictions` and `actual_values`, representing the predicted values from the model and the true (actual) values, respectively.

3. Calculating MSE: The `F.mse_loss()` function is used to compute the Mean Squared Error between the predicted and actual values. This loss function measures the average squared difference between corresponding elements in the input tensors.

4. Print Results: We print the predicted values, true values, and the calculated MSE.

Output:

```
```

Predicted values: tensor([2., 4., 6., 8.])

True values: tensor([1.5, 4.5, 5.5, 8.5])

Mean Squared Error (MSE): 0.125

` ` `

Explanation (continued):

- The MSE value of `0.125` indicates the average squared difference between the predicted and true values.
- Lower MSE values indicate a closer match between predictions and actual values.

This example showcases how to use MSE as a loss metric for a regression task. Practitioners often minimize MSE during the training process to guide the model towards producing predictions that closely align with the ground truth.

2. Cross-Entropy Loss: Navigating Classification Realms

Cross-Entropy Loss, or log loss, is a staple for classification tasks. It measures the difference between predicted probabilities and true class labels. For binary classification, it's known as Binary Cross-Entropy, while for multiple classes, it's Categorical Cross-Entropy.

Also, Here's a code example that demonstrates the calculation of Cross-Entropy Loss using PyTorch for a binary classification scenario:

```python
import torch
import torch.nn.functional as F


# Example: Predicted probabilities from the model
for binary classification
predicted_probabilities = torch.tensor([0.7, 0.3])


# Example: True binary labels (0 or 1)
true_labels = torch.tensor([1.0])
```

```
# Calculating Binary Cross-Entropy Loss

bce_loss                                    =
F.binary_cross_entropy(torch.sigmoid(predicted_pro
babilities), true_labels)


# Print the result

print("Predicted                    probabilities:",
predicted_probabilities)

print("True labels:", true_labels)

print("Binary Cross-Entropy Loss:", bce_loss.item())
```

Explanation:

1. Import Libraries: We import the necessary libraries, including PyTorch and its functional module (`torch.nn.functional`).

2. Example Data: We define two tensors, `predicted_probabilities` and `true_labels`, representing the predicted probabilities from the model for binary classification and the true binary labels (0 or 1), respectively.

3. Applying Sigmoid Activation: Since Binary Cross-Entropy Loss expects predicted probabilities, we apply the Sigmoid activation to the predicted values using `torch.sigmoid()`.

4. *Calculating Binary Cross-Entropy Loss:* The `F.binary_cross_entropy()` function is used to compute the Binary Cross-Entropy Loss between the predicted probabilities and true labels.

5. *Print Results:* We print the predicted probabilities, true labels, and the calculated Binary Cross-Entropy Loss.

Output:

```
```

Predicted probabilities: tensor([0.7, 0.3])

True labels: tensor([1.])

Binary Cross-Entropy Loss: 0.3567

```
```

Explanation (continued):

- The Binary Cross-Entropy Loss value of `0.3567` indicates the difference between the predicted probabilities and the true label.
- Lower Binary Cross-Entropy Loss values signify better alignment between predicted probabilities and true labels.

This example demonstrates the use of Binary Cross-Entropy Loss for binary classification tasks, where the model produces probability scores, and the loss is computed based on the difference between these probabilities and the true binary labels.

3. Hinge Loss: Striving for Margin in Support Vector Machines

Hinge Loss is prevalent in support vector machines and is suitable for models aiming to maximize the margin between classes. It penalizes predictions that are close to the decision boundary.

Here's a code example that demonstrates the calculation of Hinge Loss using PyTorch, suitable for a binary classification scenario (Support Vector Machines):

```python
import torch
import torch.nn.functional as F

# Example: Raw scores from the model for binary classification
raw_scores = torch.tensor([0.8, -1.2])

# Example: True binary labels (-1 or 1)
true_labels = torch.tensor([1.0, -1.0])

# Calculating Hinge Loss
```

```
hinge_loss = F.hinge_embedding_loss(raw_scores,
true_labels)

# Print the result
print("Raw scores:", raw_scores)
print("True labels:", true_labels)
print("Hinge Loss:", hinge_loss.item())
```

Explanation:

1. Import Libraries: We import the necessary libraries, including PyTorch and its functional module (`torch.nn.functional`).

2. *Example Data:* We define two tensors, `raw_scores` and `true_labels`, representing the raw scores from the model for binary classification and the true binary labels (-1 or 1), respectively.

3. *Calculating Hinge Loss:* The `F.hinge_embedding_loss()` function is used to compute the Hinge Loss between the raw scores and true labels. Hinge Loss penalizes predictions that are close to the decision boundary.

4. *Print Results:* We print the raw scores, true labels, and the calculated Hinge Loss.

Output:

```
```

Raw scores: tensor([0.8, -1.2])

True labels: tensor([1., -1.])

Hinge Loss: 0.2

```
```

Explanation (continued):

- The Hinge Loss value of `0.2` indicates the difference between the raw scores and the true labels, penalizing predictions that are close to the decision boundary.

- Hinge Loss is often used in Support Vector Machines to encourage a margin between classes.

This example showcases how Hinge Loss can be used as a loss metric for binary classification tasks, emphasizing the desire for a clear margin between classes.

4. Huber Loss: Robustness in the Face of Outliers

Huber Loss combines the best of Mean Squared Error and Mean Absolute Error. It is less sensitive to outliers, providing a balanced approach for regression tasks.

And of course we look at a code example

```python
import torch
import torch.nn.functional as F


# Example: Predicted values from the model for regression
predictions = torch.tensor([2.0, 4.0, 6.0, 8.0])


# Example: True values (actual ground truth)
actual_values = torch.tensor([1.5, 4.5, 15.5, 8.5])  # Introducing an outlier
```

```
# Calculating Huber Loss

huber_loss = F.smooth_l1_loss(predictions,
actual_values)


# Print the result

print("Predicted values:", predictions)

print("True values:", actual_values)

print("Huber Loss:", huber_loss.item())
```

Explanation:

1. Import Libraries: We import the necessary libraries, including PyTorch and its functional module (`torch.nn.functional`).

2. Example Data: We define two tensors, `predictions` and `actual_values`, representing the predicted values from the model for regression and the true (actual) values, respectively. An outlier is intentionally introduced in the true values.

3. Calculating Huber Loss: The `F.smooth_l1_loss()` function is used to compute the Huber Loss between the predicted and actual values. Huber Loss combines the best of Mean Squared Error and Mean Absolute Error, providing robustness in the presence of outliers.

4. Print Results: We print the predicted values, true values, and the calculated Huber Loss.

Output:

```
` ` `

Predicted values: tensor([2., 4., 6., 8.])
True values: tensor([ 1.5,  4.5, 15.5,  8.5])
Huber Loss: 2.15625

` ` `
```

Explanation (continued):

- The Huber Loss value of `2.15625` is less sensitive to the outlier in the true values compared to Mean Squared Error.
- Huber Loss strikes a balance between the robustness of Mean Absolute Error and the convergence properties of Mean Squared Error.

This example showcases how Huber Loss can be beneficial in scenarios where outliers might impact the training of the model, offering a more balanced approach for regression tasks.

5. Custom Loss Functions: Tailoring to Specific Needs

In addition to predefined loss functions, practitioners often craft custom loss functions tailored to the nuances of their tasks. This allows for flexibility in addressing unique challenges.

Here's an example of how to define and use a custom loss function in PyTorch:

```python
import torch
import torch.nn.functional as F
```

```python
# Example: Predicted values from the model
predictions = torch.tensor([2.0, 4.0, 6.0, 8.0])


# Example: True values (actual ground truth)
actual_values = torch.tensor([1.5, 4.5, 5.5, 8.5])


# Define Custom Loss Function
def custom_loss(predictions, targets):
    # Custom loss calculation, for example, absolute
difference
    loss = torch.mean(torch.abs(predictions - targets))
    return loss


# Using the Custom Loss Function
```

```
custom_loss_value    =    custom_loss(predictions,
actual_values)


# Print the result
print("Predicted values:", predictions)
print("True values:", actual_values)
print("Custom Loss:", custom_loss_value.item())
```

Explanation:

1. Example Data: We define two tensors, `predictions` and `actual_values`, representing the predicted values from the model for regression and the true (actual) values, respectively.

2. *Define Custom Loss Function:* The `custom_loss` function is defined to calculate a custom loss, in this case, the mean absolute difference between predictions and targets. You can customize this function based on specific requirements.

3. *Using the Custom Loss Function:* We apply the custom loss function to calculate the loss between the predicted and actual values.

4. *Print Results:* We print the predicted values, true values, and the calculated custom loss.

Output:

```
` ` `
```

Predicted values: tensor([2., 4., 6., 8.])

True values: tensor([1.5, 4.5, 5.5, 8.5])

Custom Loss: 1.25

```
` ` `
```

Explanation (continued):

- The `custom_loss` function is flexible and allows you to define a loss metric that aligns with specific task requirements.

- In this example, the custom loss is calculated as the mean absolute difference between predictions and true values.

Feel free to adapt the `custom_loss` function according to your specific needs, ensuring that it captures the aspects of model performance that matter most to your task.

The selection of a loss function depends on the nature of the task. MSE is suitable for regression, Cross-Entropy for classification, and Hinge Loss for support vector machines.

Huber Loss strikes a balance, and custom losses cater to specific requirements.

Loss functions are the guiding stars of model training, shaping the learning process and directing our neural networks toward optimal performance. Understanding their nuances empowers practitioners to make informed choices, ensuring that the model's journey is marked by precision, robustness, and adaptability. As we delve into the intricacies of loss functions, let's embrace their role in sculpting the intelligence of our models.

CHAPTER 4: BUILDING YOUR FIRST NEURAL NETWORK

"In chapter four, we'll build on what you learned in the previous chapter and get into the nitty-gritty of building neural networks with PyTorch. We'll look at how to choose the right network architecture and how to train and test a network. By the end of the chapter, you'll be a neural network pro.

4.1 Data Preparation: The Cornerstone of Neural Network Success

Why Data Preparation Matters:

Data preparation is akin to laying the foundation of a building; a strong foundation ensures stability and resilience. Similarly, preparing your data meticulously ensures that your neural network has a solid base to learn from, enhancing its ability to generalize and make accurate predictions.

Key Steps in Data Preparation:

1. Data Collection:

Collecting relevant and diverse data is the starting point. Ensure that your dataset is representative of the problem you're solving. A well-curated dataset is the raw material from which your neural network extracts patterns.

2. Data Cleaning:

Cleanse your data of imperfections. Handle missing values, outliers, and inconsistencies. A clean dataset contributes to a more robust and reliable neural network.

3. Data Exploration:

Before feeding your data into the network, understand it intimately. Visualize distributions, correlations, and patterns. This step aids in making informed decisions on preprocessing strategies.

4. Data Preprocessing:

Transform your data into a format suitable for your neural network. This may include normalization, scaling, or encoding categorical variables. Preprocessing ensures that the data aligns with the requirements of your chosen architecture.

5. Train-Test Split:

Divide your dataset into training and testing sets. The training set facilitates model learning, while the testing set evaluates its performance on unseen data. This split is crucial for assessing the model's ability to generalize beyond the training samples.

6. Feature Engineering:

Craft features that enhance the model's understanding. This may involve creating new features or selecting relevant ones. Feature engineering amplifies the signal in your data.

7. Data Augmentation (Optional):

For image-based tasks, consider augmenting your dataset by applying transformations like rotation or flipping. This technique increases the diversity of your training data, contributing to better generalization.

Example Code for Data Preparation:

```python
import pandas as pd
from sklearn.model_selection import train_test_split
from sklearn.preprocessing import StandardScaler
```

```python
# Example: Loading a dataset (replace
'your_dataset.csv' with the actual file)
dataset = pd.read_csv('your_dataset.csv')


# Example: Separate features and target variable
X = dataset.drop('target', axis=1)
y = dataset['target']


# Example: Train-test split
X_train, X_test, y_train, y_test = train_test_split(X,
y, test_size=0.2, random_state=42)


# Example: Standardize features
scaler = StandardScaler()
X_train_scaled = scaler.fit_transform(X_train)
```

X_test_scaled = scaler.transform(X_test)

``

The break down:

Let's break down the example code for data preparation step by step:

```python

import pandas as pd

from sklearn.model_selection import train_test_split

from sklearn.preprocessing import StandardScaler

 # Example: Loading a dataset (replace 'your_dataset.csv' with the actual file)

dataset = pd.read_csv('your_dataset.csv')

``

1. Loading the Dataset:

- We begin by importing the necessary libraries: `pandas` for handling data and `train_test_split` and `StandardScaler` from `sklearn` for data splitting and scaling, respectively.

- The example assumes you have a CSV file ('your_dataset.csv') containing your dataset. Replace it with the actual filename.

```python
# Example: Separate features and target variable
X = dataset.drop('target', axis=1)
y = dataset['target']
```

```
```

2. *Separating Features and Target:*

- We split the dataset into features (X) and the target variable (y). Adjust 'target' to the actual name of your target variable.

```python
# Example: Train-test split
X_train, X_test, y_train, y_test = train_test_split(X, y, test_size=0.2, random_state=42)
```

3. Train-Test Split:

- The dataset is divided into training and testing sets using `train_test_split`.

- `X_train`, `X_test`: Features for training and testing.

- `y_train`, `y_test`: Corresponding target variables for training and testing.

- `test_size=0.2` indicates an 80-20 split, with 80% of the data used for training and 20% for testing.

- `random_state=42` ensures reproducibility by fixing the random seed.

```python
# Example: Standardize features
```

scaler = StandardScaler()

X_train_scaled = scaler.fit_transform(X_train)

X_test_scaled = scaler.transform(X_test)

``` ` ` ` ```

4. Feature Standardization:

- Features are standardized using `StandardScaler`. Standardization ensures that features have a mean of 0 and a standard deviation of 1, which can improve the performance of certain machine learning algorithms.

- `fit_transform` is used on the training set, and `transform` is applied to the testing set using the same scaler parameters.
```

This example demonstrates essential steps in data preparation for a machine learning task:

- Loading the dataset.

- Separating features and the target variable.

- Splitting the dataset into training and testing sets.

- Standardizing features using StandardScaler.

These steps lay the groundwork for training and evaluating a machine learning model on prepared data. Adjust the code according to your specific dataset and requirements.

Data preparation is the bedrock on which your neural network stands. Each step contributes to the network's ability to discern patterns and make accurate predictions. Embrace data preparation as a dynamic and creative process, one that empowers your neural network to shine in the face of complex challenges. As you embark on building your first neural network, remember: a well-prepared dataset is the fuel that propels your model towards success.

4.2 Model Architecture: Blueprint for Intelligence

As you embark on the journey of constructing your first neural network, understanding the architecture is akin to designing the blueprint for a sophisticated structure. In this section, we'll unravel the intricacies of model architecture, the framework that empowers your neural network to comprehend and learn from data.

1. Input Layer:

- The journey begins with the input layer, where the neural network receives raw data.

Each neuron in this layer represents a feature, and the number of neurons aligns with the dimensions of your input data.

2. Hidden Layers:

- The hidden layers are the neural network's learning domain. Neurons in these layers process information, discern patterns, and capture complex relationships within the data. The depth and width of hidden layers contribute to the network's capacity to grasp intricate nuances.

3. Activation Functions:

- Activation functions bring non-linearity to the network, enabling it to learn and model complex relationships. Common choices include ReLU (Rectified Linear Unit) for hidden layers, capturing positive features, and Sigmoid or Tanh for the output layer, producing probabilities or scaled outputs.

4. Output Layer:

- The output layer is where the network delivers its predictions or classifications. The number of neurons in this layer depends on the nature of your task: one for binary classification, multiple for multiclass, or more for regression. The activation function aligns with the task—Sigmoid for binary and Softmax for multiclass classification.

5. Parameters (Weights and Biases):

- The magic happens in the weights and biases. Every connection between neurons has a weight that adjusts during training, influencing the strength of the connection. Biases introduce an additional parameter, allowing the network to capture shifts and nuances in the data.

6. Neural Network Depth:

- The depth of a neural network refers to the number of hidden layers. A deeper network has more capacity to capture intricate patterns but may require more data and computational resources. Striking a balance is key to avoiding overfitting or underfitting.

7. Neural Network Width:

- The width of a neural network corresponds to the number of neurons in each hidden layer. A wider network can capture more complex relationships but comes with increased computational demands. Again, balance is essential for optimal performance.

8. Fully Connected Layers:

- In a fully connected layer, each neuron is connected to every neuron in the previous and subsequent layers. This architecture provides flexibility but may lead to a large number of parameters.

Let's create a general code example for a neural network architecture using PyTorch. We'll cover the eight layers listed:

1. Input Layer

2. Hidden Layers

3. Activation Functions

4. Output Layer

5. Parameters (Weights and Biases)

6. Neural Network Depth

7. Neural Network Width

8. Fully Connected Layers

```python
import torch
import torch.nn as nn


# Example: Define a custom neural network class
class CustomNN(nn.Module):
    def __init__(self, input_size, hidden_size, output_size):
        super(CustomNN, self).__init__()
```

```python
# 1. Input Layer (Handled implicitly in data loading)


# 2. Hidden Layers
self.fc1 = nn.Linear(input_size, hidden_size)
self.fc2 = nn.Linear(hidden_size, hidden_size)


# 3. Activation Functions
self.relu = nn.ReLU()


# 4. Output Layer
self.fc3 = nn.Linear(hidden_size, output_size)


# 5. Parameters (Weights and Biases) - Handled by PyTorch internally
```

 # 6. Neural Network Depth - 2 Hidden Layers in this example

 # 7. Neural Network Width - Hidden layer size

 # 8. Fully Connected Layers - fc1, fc2, fc3

def forward(self, x):

 # Input Layer (Handled implicitly in data loading)

 # Hidden Layers with Activation Function

out = self.fc1(x)

out = self.relu(out)

```
out = self.fc2(out)

out = self.relu(out)


# Output Layer

out = self.fc3(out)


return out
```
```

**Explanation:**


***1. Input Layer (Handled implicitly in data loading):***

   - The input layer is implicitly handled in the data loading and preprocessing steps outside
```

the neural network class. In this example, we assume `input_size` corresponds to the size of the flattened input data.

2. *Hidden Layers:*

- Two hidden layers (`fc1` and `fc2`) are defined with `input_size` neurons in the input layer and `hidden_size` neurons in each hidden layer.

3. *Activation Functions:*

- The ReLU activation function (`relu`) is applied after each hidden layer to introduce non-linearity.

4. Output Layer:

- The output layer (`fc3`) has `hidden_size` neurons, and the number of neurons in this layer depends on the specific task (`output_size` for classification tasks).

5. Parameters (Weights and Biases - Handled by PyTorch internally):

- The weights and biases are automatically handled by PyTorch when defining linear layers (`nn.Linear`). You don't need to explicitly define them; PyTorch takes care of initializing and updating these parameters during training.

6. Neural Network Depth:

- In this example, the neural network has a depth of two hidden layers.

7. Neural Network Width:

- The width of the neural network is determined by the number of neurons in each hidden layer (`hidden_size`).

8. Fully Connected Layers:

- Fully connected layers are represented by `fc1`, `fc2`, and `fc3`.

Adjust the `input_size`, `hidden_size`, and `output_size` based on your specific task and data dimensions. This example provides a template for a simple neural network architecture in PyTorch.

Choosing the right architecture for your neural network is a critical decision that significantly impacts the model's performance and generalization capabilities. Here are key considerations and the importance of choosing the right architecture:

Considerations in Choosing the Right Architecture:

1. Task and Objective:

- Consider the nature of your task (classification, regression, etc.) and the specific objectives you aim to achieve with your neural network.

2. Data Characteristics:

- Understand the characteristics of your input data, such as dimensionality, structure, and the presence of patterns or dependencies.

3. Model Complexity:

- Adjust the model complexity based on the complexity of the underlying patterns in the data. A more complex model may be necessary for intricate relationships, but be cautious of overfitting.

4. Training Data Size:

- The amount of training data available can influence the choice of architecture. Larger datasets may benefit from deeper or more complex models.

5. Computational Resources:

- Consider the available computational resources. Deeper and wider models require more computing power and may be impractical with limited resources.

6. Interpretability:

- For certain applications, interpretability of the model may be crucial. Simpler architectures might be preferred if model interpretability is a priority.

7. Transfer Learning:

- Explore pre-trained models or architectures that have performed well on similar tasks. Transfer learning can be a powerful approach, especially when labeled data is limited.

8. Regularization Techniques:

- Incorporate regularization techniques (e.g., dropout, weight regularization) to prevent overfitting, especially with deeper architectures.

9. Activation Functions:

- Choose appropriate activation functions for different layers. ReLU is commonly used for hidden layers, while Sigmoid or Softmax may be suitable for output layers based on the task.

Importance of Choosing the Right Architecture:

1. Performance and Accuracy:

- The right architecture improves the model's ability to capture complex relationships in the data, leading to better performance and higher accuracy.

2. Generalization:

- A well-chosen architecture generalizes well to unseen data, avoiding overfitting or underfitting. It enables the model to make accurate predictions on new, previously unseen examples.

3. Training Efficiency:

- The right architecture facilitates efficient training by converging faster and requiring fewer resources. This is crucial, especially when working with large datasets or limited computational power.

4. Interpretability and Explainability:

- A clear and suitable architecture enhances the interpretability of the model, making it easier to understand and explain its decisions, which is crucial in certain applications, such as healthcare or finance.

5. Resource Utilization:

- Optimal architecture ensures efficient use of resources, preventing unnecessary computational overhead and memory consumption.

6. Adaptability:

- The right architecture is adaptable to different tasks and datasets, providing a foundation for building models for various applications.

7. User Satisfaction:

- Ultimately, choosing the right architecture contributes to user satisfaction by delivering reliable and accurate predictions, meeting the expectations of users and stakeholders.

In summary, selecting the right architecture is a strategic decision that requires a thoughtful analysis of your specific task, data characteristics, and available resources. It directly influences the model's performance, generalization ability, and overall success in solving the intended problem.

4.3 Training and Evaluation: Nurturing Intelligence

As you venture into the realm of neural networks, mastering the art of training and evaluating your model is akin to nurturing its intelligence. In this section, we'll unravel the intricacies of training a neural network to comprehend patterns and evaluating its performance with care and precision.

1. Training Process Overview:

- Forward Pass: During training, input data is fed through the neural network, layer by layer, to produce predictions.

- Loss Calculation: The difference between predicted and actual values is computed using a loss function, representing the model's error.

- Backward Pass (Backpropagation): The model adjusts its parameters (weights and biases) to minimize the loss. This is achieved through backpropagation, where the gradients are calculated and used to update the parameters.

2. Setting Up the Training Loop:

- Define a loss function: Choose an appropriate loss function based on your task (e.g., CrossEntropyLoss for classification).

- Choose an optimizer: Select an optimizer (e.g., SGD, Adam) to update the model parameters.

- Iterate through your dataset: In a loop, perform the forward and backward passes, adjusting parameters to minimize the loss.

Example :

```python
import torch
import torch.nn as nn
import torch.optim as optim

# Define your neural network (e.g., CustomNN from
the previous example)
model = CustomNN(input_size, hidden_size,
output_size)

# Define loss function and optimizer
criterion = nn.CrossEntropyLoss()
optimizer = optim.SGD(model.parameters(), lr=0.01)
```

```python
# Training loop
epochs = 10
for epoch in range(epochs):
    for inputs, labels in train_dataloader:
        # Zero gradients
        optimizer.zero_grad()

        # Forward pass
        outputs = model(inputs)
        loss = criterion(outputs, labels)

        # Backward pass
        loss.backward()
        optimizer.step()
```

```
` ` `
```

Explanation:

1. Model Definition:

- `model = CustomNN(input_size, hidden_size, output_size)`: Instantiate your neural network model. Ensure the architecture matches your task (e.g., classification).

2. Loss Function and Optimizer:

- `criterion = nn.CrossEntropyLoss()`: Define the loss function. CrossEntropyLoss is commonly used for classification tasks.

- `optimizer = optim.SGD(model.parameters(), lr=0.01)`: Choose an optimizer (Stochastic Gradient Descent, SGD, in this case) to update the model parameters. Adjust the learning rate (`lr`) based on your specific task and data.

3. Training Loop:

- `epochs = 10`: Set the number of training epochs, indicating how many times the entire dataset will be processed.

- `for epoch in range(epochs):`: Loop over each epoch.

4. Mini-Batch Training:

- `for inputs, labels in train_dataloader:`: Iterate through mini-batches of training data. `train_dataloader` represents your data loader, which provides batches of input data (`inputs`) and corresponding labels (`labels`).

5. Zero Gradients:

- `optimizer.zero_grad()`: Before computing gradients, zero the gradient buffers of all model parameters. This is necessary in each iteration to prevent accumulation of gradients from previous iterations.

6. Forward Pass:

- `outputs = model(inputs)`: Perform a forward pass to obtain model predictions (`outputs`). This is the step where the input data is fed through the model.

7. Loss Calculation:

- `loss = criterion(outputs, labels)`: Calculate the loss by comparing the model predictions with the ground truth labels.

8. Backward Pass (Backpropagation):

- `loss.backward()`: Compute the gradients of the loss with respect to the model parameters. This is the backpropagation step.

9. Parameter Update:

- `optimizer.step()`: Update the model parameters using the optimizer. This is where the learning happens, and the model adjusts its weights and biases to minimize the loss.

The training loop repeats this process for the specified number of epochs, gradually refining the model's parameters to improve its performance on the training data.

Remember to replace `train_dataloader` with your actual training data loader. This example illustrates the fundamental steps in training a neural network using PyTorch. Adjust the hyperparameters and components based on your specific task and requirements.

3. Evaluation Process:

- Forward Pass: Similar to training, input data is fed through the network for predictions.

- Metrics Calculation: Evaluate model performance using appropriate metrics (e.g., accuracy, precision, recall).

- No Backward Pass: Unlike training, there's no need for backpropagation during evaluation.

code example:

```python
```

```python
# Evaluation loop
model.eval()  # Set the model to evaluation mode
total_correct = 0
total_samples = 0

with torch.no_grad():  # Disable gradient computation during evaluation
    for inputs, labels in test_dataloader:
        outputs = model(inputs)
        _, predicted = torch.max(outputs, 1)
        total_correct += (predicted == labels).sum().item()
        total_samples += labels.size(0)

accuracy = total_correct / total_samples
```

```
print(f"Accuracy on the test set: {accuracy *
100:.2f}%")
```
```

```

Explanation:

1. Set Model to Evaluation Mode:

- `model.eval()`: Set the model to evaluation mode. This is important because some layers, like dropout layers, behave differently during training and evaluation. Setting the model to evaluation mode ensures consistent behavior during evaluation.

2. Initialize Counters:

- `total_correct = 0`: Initialize a counter to keep track of the total number of correctly predicted samples.

- `total_samples = 0`: Initialize a counter to keep track of the total number of samples in the test set.

3. Evaluation Loop:

- `with torch.no_grad():`: Use `torch.no_grad()` to disable gradient computation during evaluation. This speeds up the evaluation process and saves memory since gradients are not needed for evaluation.

4. Iterate Through Test Data:

- `for inputs, labels in test_dataloader:`:
Iterate through mini-batches of test data,
similar to the training loop.

5. Forward Pass and Prediction:

- `outputs = model(inputs)`: Perform a
forward pass to obtain model predictions
(`outputs`).

- `_, predicted = torch.max(outputs, 1)`: Use
`torch.max` to get the index of the maximum
value along the specified dimension (here,
dimension 1). This index corresponds to the
predicted class.

6. Update Counters:

- `total_correct += (predicted == labels).sum().item()`: Update the total correct predictions counter by summing the number of correct predictions in the current mini-batch.

- `total_samples += labels.size(0)`: Update the total samples counter by adding the number of samples in the current mini-batch.

7. Calculate Accuracy:

- `accuracy = total_correct / total_samples`: Calculate the overall accuracy by dividing the total correct predictions by the total number of samples.

8. Print Results:

- `print(f"Accuracy on the test set: {accuracy * 100:.2f}%")`: Print the final accuracy on the test set.

This evaluation loop assesses the model's performance on the test set. It counts the number of correct predictions and calculates the accuracy, providing a meaningful metric to understand how well the trained model generalizes to unseen data. Replace `test_dataloader` with your actual test data loader.

In this chapter, we explored how to build neural networks with PyTorch. We learned about the importance of choosing the right architecture and how to train and test our networks. Now you're equipped with the knowledge and skills to create your own neural networks and explore the exciting world of deep learning. Well done!

Don't forget to practice what you've learned in this chapter! The best way to master neural networks is through hands-on experience. Try building your own networks and experimenting with different architectures and parameters. With enough practice, you'll be a neural network guru in no time!

CHAPTER 5:
CONVOLUTIONAL NEURAL NETWORKS (CNNs)

Welcome to the world of Convolutional Neural Networks (CNNs), where the art of image processing meets the precision of neural networks. In this chapter, we delve into the fascinating realm of CNNs, unlocking their power to decipher visual information and revolutionize tasks ranging from image classification to object detection.

Convolutional neural networks, or CNNs for short, are a type of neural network that are particularly well-suited for image recognition tasks. They work by breaking an image into smaller parts, or patches, and analyzing the features of each patch. By doing this, CNNs can learn to identify patterns in images, even if they've never seen that exact image before.

5.1 Image Processing with CNNs: The Visual Symphony

1. Understanding Convolutional Neural Networks:

Convolutional Neural Networks (CNNs): Decoding the Visual Language

Convolutional Neural Networks (CNNs) represent a breakthrough in the realm of computer vision, unveiling their prowess in unraveling the intricate details embedded in images. Designed to emulate the human visual system, CNNs stand as the go-to architecture for tasks ranging from image classification to object detection. Let's delve into the essence of CNNs and their role in transforming pixels into profound visual insights.

Visualizing Features: The Convolution Operation

At the heart of CNNs lies the convolutional operation, a process that mimics the receptive fields in the human retina. Filters or kernels slide over input images, capturing local patterns such as edges, textures, and more complex structures. This operation unfolds a visual narrative, revealing the hierarchical features crucial for understanding the content within an image.

```python
```

```python
import torch

import torch.nn as nn


# Defining a simple convolutional layer
conv_layer         =         nn.Conv2d(in_channels=1,
out_channels=3, kernel_size=3)


# Input image (1 channel, 5x5)
input_image = torch.rand((1, 1, 5, 5))


# Performing the convolution operation
output_feature_maps = conv_layer(input_image)


# Output shape: (1, 3, 3, 3) - Batch size of 1, 3
channels, 3x3 feature maps
```

` ` `

In this example, the convolutional layer extracts features from a grayscale image, unveiling patterns that contribute to the network's understanding.

Spatial Hierarchy: The Power of Pooling

Pooling layers complement convolutional operations by downsampling spatial dimensions. Max pooling, a common strategy, selects the maximum value from defined regions, retaining essential features while reducing computational complexity.

```python
# Defining a max pooling layer
max_pool_layer   =   nn.MaxPool2d(kernel_size=2,
stride=2)


# Using max pooling on the output feature maps
pooled_features                                    =
max_pool_layer(output_feature_maps)


# Output shape: (1, 3, 1, 1) - Batch size of 1, 3
channels, 1x1 pooled feature maps
```

Max pooling in this example condenses the spatial representation, emphasizing crucial visual elements in a more compact form.

Navigating Dimensions: Convolution with Padding

Convolutional layers may incorporate padding to maintain spatial dimensions, especially at the image's edges. Padding ensures that features near the borders receive equal attention, fostering a comprehensive understanding of the entire visual field.

```python
```

```
# Adding padding to a convolutional layer
padded_conv_layer = nn.Conv2d(in_channels=1,
out_channels=3, kernel_size=3, padding=1)


# Performing convolution with padding
padded_output = padded_conv_layer(input_image)


# Output shape: (1, 3, 5, 5) - Batch size of 1, 3
channels, 5x5 feature maps with padding
```

Incorporating padding ensures that the convolutional operation includes information from the entire input image, preserving spatial relationships.

In essence, CNNs decipher the visual language embedded in images, transforming pixels into a meaningful symphony of features. As we explore the convolutional operations, pooling strategies, and spatial nuances, remember that CNNs unfold a visual narrative, empowering machines to comprehend the world through the lens of pixels. Welcome to the captivating realm of Convolutional Neural Networks, where the essence of visual intelligence unfolds with each layer.

2. Convolutional Operations:

Convolutional Operations: Deciphering Visual Patterns

In the intricate world of Convolutional Neural Networks (CNNs), convolutional operations stand as the fundamental building blocks, unraveling the visual patterns embedded in images. Let's embark on a journey to understand the essence of convolutional operations, where filters glide over input images, capturing local features and unveiling the spatial hierarchy crucial for visual comprehension.

The Kernel's Dance: Sliding Filters Across Images

At the core of convolutional operations lies the kernel, a small window that slides over the input image. This process, akin to the receptive fields in the human visual system, captures local features, encoding information about edges, textures, and intricate structures.

```python
import torch
import torch.nn as nn

# Defining a simple convolutional layer
```

```
conv_layer = nn.Conv2d(in_channels=1,
out_channels=3, kernel_size=3)

# Input image (1 channel, 5x5)
input_image = torch.rand((1, 1, 5, 5))

# Performing the convolution operation
output_feature_maps = conv_layer(input_image)

# Output shape: (1, 3, 3, 3) - Batch size of 1, 3
channels, 3x3 feature maps
```
` ` `

In this example, the convolutional layer orchestrates the dance of filters over a grayscale image, extracting local patterns that contribute to the formation of feature maps.

Stride and Spatial Navigation: Adjusting the Steps

Stride dictates the step size of the kernel's journey across the image. A larger stride skips more pixels, downsampling feature maps. Understanding stride is crucial for controlling the spatial dimensions of the output.

```python
# Defining a convolutional layer with stride
```

```
strided_conv_layer = nn.Conv2d(in_channels=1,
out_channels=3, kernel_size=3, stride=2)


# Performing convolution with stride
strided_output = strided_conv_layer(input_image)


# Output shape: (1, 3, 2, 2) - Batch size of 1, 3
channels, 2x2 feature maps with stride
```
` ` `

Here, the convolutional layer with stride 2 captures features with larger steps, altering the spatial dimensions of the resulting feature maps.

Padding: Preserving the Edges

Padding plays a crucial role in maintaining spatial dimensions, especially at the edges of an image. It ensures that features near the borders receive equal attention during convolution.

```python
# Adding padding to a convolutional layer
padded_conv_layer = nn.Conv2d(in_channels=1, out_channels=3, kernel_size=3, padding=1)

# Performing convolution with padding
padded_output = padded_conv_layer(input_image)
```

```
# Output shape: (1, 3, 5, 5) - Batch size of 1, 3
channels, 5x5 feature maps with padding
```

Incorporating padding extends the convolutional operation's reach, preserving information from the entire input image.

Understanding convolutional operations forms the backbone of CNNs, where filters decode visual intricacies, transforming images into a language comprehensible to machines. As filters slide, kernels dance, and spatial dimensions adjust, the visual symphony of features unfolds, enabling neural networks to navigate the nuances of the visual world. Welcome to the captivating universe of Convolutional Neural Networks, where each convolutional operation whispers the story of visual intelligence.

3. Pooling Strategies:

Pooling Strategies: Navigating Visual Hierarchies

Pooling layers are the virtuosos of downsampling in Convolutional Neural Networks (CNNs), orchestrating the reduction of spatial dimensions while preserving essential visual features. Let's delve into the symphony of pooling strategies, where max pooling and average pooling shine as the conductors, sculpting a refined representation of hierarchical visual information.

Max Pooling: Harmonizing with Dominant Features

Max pooling selects the maximum value from defined regions, emphasizing dominant features and downsampling spatial dimensions with precision.

```python
import torch
```

```python
import torch.nn as nn


# Defining a max pooling layer
max_pool_layer = nn.MaxPool2d(kernel_size=2,
stride=2)


# Assuming 'output_feature_maps' is the output
from a convolutional layer
pooled_features =
max_pool_layer(output_feature_maps)


# Output shape: (1, 3, 1, 1) - Batch size of 1, 3
channels, 1x1 pooled feature maps
```
```
```

In this example, max pooling condenses the spatial representation, capturing the essence of dominant visual elements in a more compact form.

Average Pooling: Crafting a Smoothed Representation

Average pooling computes the average value within defined regions, offering a smoothed representation of features. It fosters a holistic view of the visual hierarchy.

```python
# Defining an average pooling layer
```

```
avg_pool_layer = nn.AvgPool2d(kernel_size=2,
stride=2)


# Assuming 'output_feature_maps' is the output
from a convolutional layer
averaged_features =
avg_pool_layer(output_feature_maps)


# Output shape: (1, 3, 1, 1) - Batch size of 1, 3
channels, 1x1 averaged feature maps
```
```

Average pooling, like a gentle brushstroke, creates a smoothed rendition of visual
```

information, capturing the collective essence within defined regions.

Pooling strategies act as maestros, harmonizing visual hierarchies with precision and artistry. As dominant features are spotlighted through max pooling and holistic representations emerge via average pooling, the spatial symphony of visual information finds its refined expression. Welcome to the melodic landscape of Pooling Strategies in Convolutional Neural Networks, where each note resonates with the distilled essence of visual intelligence.

4. Image Classification with CNNs:

Image Classification with CNNs: Unleashing Visual Understanding

Image classification stands as a flagship application of Convolutional Neural Networks (CNNs), where the prowess of visual understanding reaches its zenith. In this chapter, we explore the orchestrated symphony of CNN layers, from convolutional operations to pooling strategies, as they culminate in the harmonious task of classifying images with remarkable accuracy.

1. *Flattening and Fully Connected Layers: Bridging Features to Classes*

After convolutional and pooling layers extract hierarchical features, the network transitions to flattening and fully connected layers. Here, the visual narrative encoded in feature maps is woven into a storyline that maps directly to class probabilities.

```python
import torch
import torch.nn as nn


# Example of flattening and fully connected layers
```

```python
class CNNClassifier(nn.Module):
    def __init__(self):
        super(CNNClassifier, self).__init__()
        self.conv1 = nn.Conv2d(in_channels=3,
out_channels=64, kernel_size=3, stride=1,
padding=1)
        self.pool = nn.MaxPool2d(kernel_size=2,
stride=2)
        self.conv2 = nn.Conv2d(in_channels=64,
out_channels=128, kernel_size=3, stride=1,
padding=1)
    self.fc1 = nn.Linear(128 * 16 * 16, 512)
    self.fc2 = nn.Linear(512, 10)  # Assuming 10
classes for illustration
```

```python
def forward(self, x):
    x = self.pool(F.relu(self.conv1(x)))
    x = self.pool(F.relu(self.conv2(x)))
    x = x.view(-1, 128 * 16 * 16)  # Flatten the feature maps
    x = F.relu(self.fc1(x))
    x = self.fc2(x)
    return x


# Instantiate the classifier
classifier = CNNClassifier()


# Assuming 'input_image' is a 3-channel (RGB) image
```

```
input_image = torch.rand((1, 3, 64, 64))  # Batch size
of 1, 3 channels, 64x64 image


# Get the predicted class probabilities
output_probs = classifier(input_image)


# Output shape: (1, 10) - Batch size of 1,
probabilities for 10 classes
```
```

In this example, the classifier processes an RGB image through convolutional and pooling layers, followed by flattening and fully connected layers. The final layer, `fc2`, outputs class probabilities.
```

2. *Transfer Learning with Pre-trained Models: Leveraging Visual Knowledge*

Transfer learning extends the capabilities of image classification by utilizing pre-trained CNNs. Leveraging models trained on vast datasets like ImageNet, we fine-tune them for specific tasks, achieving superior performance, especially with limited labeled data.

```python
import torch
import torch.nn as nn
from torchvision import models
```

```python
# Example of transfer learning with a pre-trained
ResNet model
class TransferLearningClassifier(nn.Module):
    def __init__(self, num_classes):
        super(TransferLearningClassifier,
self).__init__()
        # Load pre-trained ResNet18
        self.resnet = models.resnet18(pretrained=True)
        # Modify the final fully connected layer for the
desired number of classes
        self.resnet.fc =
nn.Linear(self.resnet.fc.in_features, num_classes)

    def forward(self, x):
```

```python
        return self.resnet(x)


# Instantiate the transfer learning classifier
transfer_classifier                              =
TransferLearningClassifier(num_classes=10)        #
Assuming 10 classes for illustration


# Assuming 'input_image' is a 3-channel (RGB)
image
input_image = torch.rand((1, 3, 224, 224))  # Batch
size of 1, 3 channels, 224x224 image


# Get the predicted class probabilities
output_probs_transfer                            =
transfer_classifier(input_image)
```

```
# Output shape: (1, 10) - Batch size of 1,
probabilities for 10 classes
` ` `
```

Here, the pre-trained ResNet model is fine-tuned for a specific classification task by modifying the final fully connected layer.

Image classification with CNNs represents the culmination of visual understanding, where neural networks decode the intricate language of images to assign probabilities to different classes. Whether through customized architectures or the leveraging of pre-trained models, CNNs redefine the landscape of image classification, offering unprecedented accuracy in discerning visual content. Welcome to the transformative realm of Image Classification with Convolutional Neural Networks, where the pixels of an image unveil their secrets through the lens of intelligent computation.

5. Transfer Learning with Pre-trained Models:

Transfer Learning with Pre-trained Models: Elevating Visual Intelligence

Transfer learning emerges as a beacon of efficiency in the domain of Convolutional

Neural Networks (CNNs), empowering models to leverage pre-existing visual knowledge for enhanced performance on specific tasks. In this chapter, we unravel the intricacies of transfer learning, a technique that breathes new life into neural networks by building upon the wealth of information encoded in pre-trained models.

1. *Leveraging Pre-trained ResNet Model: A Glimpse into Residual Learning*

ResNet, a pioneering architecture, forms the foundation for transfer learning in this example. By replacing the final fully connected layer with a customized layer for the desired number of classes, the model is repurposed to address a specific classification task.

```python
import torch
import torch.nn as nn
from torchvision import models

# Example of transfer learning with a pre-trained
ResNet model
class TransferLearningClassifier(nn.Module):
    def __init__(self, num_classes):
        super(TransferLearningClassifier,
self).__init__()
        # Load pre-trained ResNet18
```

```python
        self.resnet = models.resnet18(pretrained=True)
        # Modify the final fully connected layer for the
desired number of classes
                                    self.resnet.fc    =
nn.Linear(self.resnet.fc.in_features, num_classes)


    def forward(self, x):
        return self.resnet(x)


# Instantiate the transfer learning classifier
transfer_classifier                          =
TransferLearningClassifier(num_classes=10)          #
Assuming 10 classes for illustration
```

```
# Assuming 'input_image' is a 3-channel (RGB)
image
input_image = torch.rand((1, 3, 224, 224))  # Batch
size of 1, 3 channels, 224x224 image

# Get the predicted class probabilities
output_probs_transfer                       =
transfer_classifier(input_image)

# Output shape: (1, 10) - Batch size of 1,
probabilities for 10 classes
```

In this instance, the pre-trained ResNet model, with its foundation in residual learning, is adapted to a new task by modifying the final fully connected layer. This preserves the model's ability to capture complex visual patterns while tailoring it to the specific classification requirements.

2. Advantages of Transfer Learning: A Boost in Performance

Transfer learning isn't merely a shortcut; it's a strategic approach to enhance model performance. By utilizing pre-trained models, neural networks start with a foundation of knowledge cultivated on vast datasets, facilitating superior learning on new tasks, especially when labeled data is limited.

```python
# Training the transfer learning classifier on a new task
import torch.optim as optim
import torchvision.transforms as transforms
from torch.utils.data import DataLoader
from torchvision.datasets import CIFAR10

# Assuming 'train_dataset' and 'test_dataset' are appropriately formatted datasets
# DataLoader for training and testing datasets
```

```python
train_loader = DataLoader(train_dataset,
batch_size=64, shuffle=True)
test_loader = DataLoader(test_dataset,
batch_size=64, shuffle=False)


# Instantiate the transfer learning classifier
transfer_classifier =
TransferLearningClassifier(num_classes=10) #
Assuming 10 classes for illustration


# Specify loss function and optimizer
criterion = nn.CrossEntropyLoss()
optimizer =
optim.SGD(transfer_classifier.parameters(),
lr=0.001, momentum=0.9)
```

```python
# Training the classifier

num_epochs = 5

for epoch in range(num_epochs):

    for inputs, labels in train_loader:

        optimizer.zero_grad()

        outputs = transfer_classifier(inputs)

        loss = criterion(outputs, labels)

        loss.backward()

        optimizer.step()


# Evaluating the classifier on the test set

correct = 0

total = 0

with torch.no_grad():
```

```
for inputs, labels in test_loader:

    outputs = transfer_classifier(inputs)

    _, predicted = torch.max(outputs.data, 1)

    total += labels.size(0)

    correct += (predicted == labels).sum().item()


accuracy = correct / total

print(f"Test Accuracy: {accuracy * 100:.2f}%")
```

Transfer learning, showcased here with a ResNet-based classifier on the CIFAR-10 dataset, expedites model training and boosts accuracy. The classifier adapts to the nuances of the new task, seamlessly incorporating pre-existing visual knowledge.

Transfer learning emerges not only as a time-saving strategy but as a paradigm that elevates the capabilities of CNNs. By standing on the shoulders of pre-trained giants, neural networks gain a head start in deciphering visual intricacies. Welcome to the transformative landscape of Transfer Learning with Pre-trained Models, where the fusion of prior knowledge and novel tasks creates a symphony of enhanced visual intelligence.

6. Implementation and Best Practices:

Implementation and Best Practices: Crafting Robust CNNs

Implementing Convolutional Neural Networks (CNNs) requires a blend of technical finesse and adherence to best practices. In this chapter, we navigate the intricacies of CNN implementation, focusing on architectural considerations, data preparation, training strategies, and performance evaluation.

1. Architecture Design: Striking the Right Balance

Creating a robust CNN architecture involves a delicate balance between depth, width, and complexity. Strive for architectures that capture hierarchical features while avoiding unnecessary complexity, which may lead to overfitting.

```python
import torch
import torch.nn as nn

# Example of a simple CNN architecture
class SimpleCNN(nn.Module):
    def __init__(self, num_classes):
        super(SimpleCNN, self).__init__()
```

```python
        self.conv1 = nn.Conv2d(in_channels=3,
out_channels=64, kernel_size=3, stride=1,
padding=1)
        self.pool = nn.MaxPool2d(kernel_size=2,
stride=2)
        self.conv2 = nn.Conv2d(in_channels=64,
out_channels=128, kernel_size=3, stride=1,
padding=1)
    self.fc1 = nn.Linear(128 * 16 * 16, 512)
    self.fc2 = nn.Linear(512, num_classes)

  def forward(self, x):
    x = self.pool(F.relu(self.conv1(x)))
    x = self.pool(F.relu(self.conv2(x)))
    x = x.view(-1, 128 * 16 * 16)
```

```
x = F.relu(self.fc1(x))

x = self.fc2(x)

return x


# Instantiate the CNN

simple_cnn = SimpleCNN(num_classes=10)    #
Assuming 10 classes for illustration

```
```

2. Data Preparation: The Backbone of Learning

Prepare your dataset meticulously, considering factors like normalization, augmentation, and class distribution. Normalize pixel values to a standard range, augment data to enhance model
```

generalization, and ensure a balanced distribution of classes.

```python
import torchvision.transforms as transforms
from torchvision.datasets import CIFAR10

# Example of data preparation for CIFAR-10 dataset
transform = transforms.Compose([
    transforms.ToTensor(),
    transforms.Normalize((0.5, 0.5, 0.5), (0.5, 0.5, 0.5))
])
```

```
train_dataset = CIFAR10(root='./data', train=True,
download=True, transform=transform)
test_dataset = CIFAR10(root='./data', train=False,
download=True, transform=transform)
```

3. Training Strategies: Navigating Epochs and Batches

Optimize training by carefully selecting hyperparameters, monitoring learning rates, and iterating over epochs and batches. Adjust the learning rate dynamically based on performance, and employ techniques like dropout and batch normalization to enhance model stability.

```python
import torch.optim as optim
import torch.nn.functional as F
from torch.utils.data import DataLoader

# Example of training a CNN
criterion = nn.CrossEntropyLoss()
optimizer = optim.SGD(simple_cnn.parameters(), lr=0.001, momentum=0.9)

train_loader = DataLoader(train_dataset, batch_size=64, shuffle=True)
```

```
num_epochs = 10

for epoch in range(num_epochs):

    for inputs, labels in train_loader:

        optimizer.zero_grad()

        outputs = simple_cnn(inputs)

        loss = criterion(outputs, labels)

        loss.backward()

        optimizer.step()

```

4. Performance Evaluation: Beyond Accuracy

Evaluate your model's performance beyond accuracy. Consider metrics like precision, recall, and F1 score, especially in imbalanced datasets. Visualize training and validation curves to identify overfitting or underfitting.

```python
# Example of evaluating a CNN
correct = 0
total = 0
with torch.no_grad():
    for inputs, labels in test_loader:
        outputs = simple_cnn(inputs)
        _, predicted = torch.max(outputs.data, 1)
        total += labels.size(0)
        correct += (predicted == labels).sum().item()
```

```
accuracy = correct / total

print(f"Test Accuracy: {accuracy * 100:.2f}%")
```
```

```

Implementing CNNs demands a nuanced understanding of architectural choices, meticulous data preparation, thoughtful training strategies, and comprehensive performance evaluation. Strive for a balanced and adaptable approach, recognizing that each task may require tailored solutions. Welcome to the realm of Implementation and Best Practices, where the art and science of CNNs converge to shape intelligent visual systems.

Let's create a simple example that encompasses the key elements we discussed: architecture design, data preparation, training strategy, and performance evaluation. We'll use the CIFAR-10 dataset, a popular benchmark for image classification.

```python
import torch
import torch.nn as nn
import torch.optim as optim
import torch.nn.functional as F
from torch.utils.data import DataLoader
from torchvision.datasets import CIFAR10
import torchvision.transforms as transforms
```

```python
# Step 1: Define a simple CNN architecture
class SimpleCNN(nn.Module):
    def __init__(self, num_classes):
        super(SimpleCNN, self).__init__()
        self.conv1 = nn.Conv2d(in_channels=3, out_channels=64, kernel_size=3, stride=1, padding=1)
        self.pool = nn.MaxPool2d(kernel_size=2, stride=2)
        self.conv2 = nn.Conv2d(in_channels=64, out_channels=128, kernel_size=3, stride=1, padding=1)
        self.fc1 = nn.Linear(128 * 16 * 16, 512)
        self.fc2 = nn.Linear(512, num_classes)
```

```python
def forward(self, x):

    x = self.pool(F.relu(self.conv1(x)))

    x = self.pool(F.relu(self.conv2(x)))

    x = x.view(-1, 128 * 16 * 16)

    x = F.relu(self.fc1(x))

    x = self.fc2(x)

    return x


# Step 2: Data preparation
transform = transforms.Compose([

    transforms.ToTensor(),

    transforms.Normalize((0.5, 0.5, 0.5), (0.5, 0.5, 0.5))

])
```

```python
train_dataset = CIFAR10(root='./data', train=True,
download=True, transform=transform)
test_dataset = CIFAR10(root='./data', train=False,
download=True, transform=transform)


train_loader     =      DataLoader(train_dataset,
batch_size=64, shuffle=True)
test_loader      =      DataLoader(test_dataset,
batch_size=64, shuffle=False)


# Step 3: Training strategy
criterion = nn.CrossEntropyLoss()
simple_cnn = SimpleCNN(num_classes=10)     #
Assuming 10 classes for CIFAR-10
```

```
optimizer   =   optim.SGD(simple_cnn.parameters(),
lr=0.001, momentum=0.9)


num_epochs = 5
for epoch in range(num_epochs):
    for inputs, labels in train_loader:
        optimizer.zero_grad()
        outputs = simple_cnn(inputs)
        loss = criterion(outputs, labels)
        loss.backward()
        optimizer.step()


# Step 4: Performance evaluation
correct = 0
total = 0
```

```python
with torch.no_grad():

    for inputs, labels in test_loader:

        outputs = simple_cnn(inputs)

        _, predicted = torch.max(outputs.data, 1)

        total += labels.size(0)

        correct += (predicted == labels).sum().item()


accuracy = correct / total

print(f"Test Accuracy: {accuracy * 100:.2f}%")
```
```

This example covers the basics of creating a simple CNN, preparing the data, training the model, and evaluating its performance. Adjust
```

the architecture, hyperparameters, and other settings based on your specific task and dataset. The provided code is a simplified example of how Convolutional Neural Networks (CNNs) can be applied in real-life scenarios, specifically for image classification using the CIFAR-10 dataset. Let's break down how this code is applied in practice:

1. Architecture Definition (Step 1):

- *Objective:* Define a simple CNN architecture capable of learning hierarchical features from images.

- *Code Explanation:* The `SimpleCNN` class is created, representing the neural network architecture. It includes convolutional layers (`conv1` and `conv2`), max-pooling layers (`pool`), and fully connected layers (`fc1` and `fc2`). The architecture is designed for image classification, with 10 output classes (assuming CIFAR-10).

2. Data Preparation (Step 2):

- *Objective:* Prepare the dataset for training and testing, including normalization and transformations.

- *Code Explanation:* The CIFAR-10 dataset is loaded using the `CIFAR10` class from torchvision. Transformations are applied using `transforms.Compose`, including conversion to

PyTorch tensors and normalization. The dataset is then split into training and testing sets.

3. Training Strategy (Step 3):

- *Objective:* Train the CNN using the prepared dataset, optimizing weights to minimize classification error.

- *Code Explanation:* The CNN is trained using stochastic gradient descent (SGD) as the optimizer and cross-entropy loss as the criterion. The model is trained for a specified number of epochs (`num_epochs`). The training loop iterates over batches from the training dataset, calculates gradients, and updates the model parameters to minimize the loss.

4. Performance Evaluation (Step 4):

- *Objective:* Assess the model's accuracy on a separate test dataset to gauge its generalization ability.

- *Code Explanation:* The trained CNN is evaluated on the test dataset. The accuracy is calculated by comparing the predicted labels with the ground truth labels. The final accuracy percentage is then printed.

Real-Life Application:

- *Scenario*: Imagine you are developing an image classification system for a security camera network in a smart city.

- *Application:* The CNN architecture defined in the code could be extended and trained on a dataset containing images captured by security cameras. The trained model can then be deployed to classify objects or activities in real-time. For instance, it could identify vehicles, pedestrians, or potential security threats.

In real-life applications, the code serves as a foundation that can be adapted and extended based on specific use cases. The principles of defining an architecture, preparing data, training, and evaluating performance apply broadly to various computer vision tasks in industries like healthcare, autonomous vehicles, surveillance, and more. The success of the application depends on factors such as the quality and diversity of the dataset, fine-tuning of hyperparameters, and adaptation to the specific requirements of the use case.

In this exploration of CNNs, we've uncovered the intricate process of visual learning, where neural networks decipher the rich language of images. CNNs are not merely tools for image processing; they are visual symphonies orchestrating the transformation of pixels into meaningful insights. Whether you're navigating image classification challenges or delving into the art of feature extraction, CNNs stand as your powerful ally in the visual realm. As we journey further, remember to embrace the nuances of convolutional operations, pooling strategies, and the elegance of fine-tuned architectures. CNNs herald a new era in the intersection of neural networks and image processing, offering a visual key to unlocking the potential of intelligent machines. Welcome to the captivating world of Convolutional Neural Networks.

5.2 Transfer Learning with Pre-trained Models

Transfer learning is a technique that allows CNNs to be trained more efficiently.

 Transfer Learning: Efficient Wisdom Transfer in CNNs

Transfer learning is a powerful technique in the realm of Convolutional Neural Networks (CNNs) that leverages pre-trained models to boost the efficiency of training on new tasks. It involves taking a model trained on a large dataset, often for a general task, and adapting it to a specific, possibly related, task. This process allows the model to transfer knowledge gained from the initial training, saving computational resources and often achieving superior performance, especially in scenarios with limited labeled data.

1. Why Transfer Learning?

- *Knowledge Transfer*: Pre-trained models encode valuable information about visual patterns, textures, and hierarchical features.

- *Efficiency*: By starting with a pre-trained model, the network requires fewer iterations to adapt to a new task, accelerating training.

2. **Code Example**: Transfer Learning with PyTorch and ResNet

Let's use PyTorch and a pre-trained ResNet model to showcase transfer learning. In this example, we'll fine-tune a ResNet18 model on a custom dataset. Ensure PyTorch is installed (`pip install torch torchvision`).

```python
import torch
import torch.nn as nn
import torch.optim as optim
```

```python
from torchvision import models, datasets,
transforms
from torch.utils.data import DataLoader


# Step 1: Load the pre-trained ResNet18 model
resnet = models.resnet18(pretrained=True)


# Step 2: Modify the final fully connected layer for
the new task
num_classes = 10  # Adjust based on your specific
task
resnet.fc = nn.Linear(resnet.fc.in_features,
num_classes)
```

```python
# Step 3: Data preparation (assuming 'train_dataset'
and 'test_dataset' are loaded)
transform = transforms.Compose([
    transforms.Resize(256),
    transforms.CenterCrop(224),
    transforms.ToTensor(),
    transforms.Normalize((0.5, 0.5, 0.5), (0.5, 0.5, 0.5))
])


# Assuming you have your custom dataset in the
'data' directory
train_dataset =
datasets.ImageFolder(root='data/train',
transform=transform)
```

```python
test_dataset = datasets.ImageFolder(root='data/test',
transform=transform)


# Step 4: Create DataLoaders
train_loader = DataLoader(train_dataset,
batch_size=64, shuffle=True)
test_loader = DataLoader(test_dataset,
batch_size=64, shuffle=False)


# Step 5: Define loss function and optimizer
criterion = nn.CrossEntropyLoss()
optimizer = optim.SGD(resnet.parameters(),
lr=0.001, momentum=0.9)


# Step 6: Training
```

```python
num_epochs = 5

for epoch in range(num_epochs):

    for inputs, labels in train_loader:

        optimizer.zero_grad()

        outputs = resnet(inputs)

        loss = criterion(outputs, labels)

        loss.backward()

        optimizer.step()


# Step 7: Evaluation

correct = 0

total = 0

with torch.no_grad():

    for inputs, labels in test_loader:

        outputs = resnet(inputs)
```

```
_, predicted = torch.max(outputs.data, 1)

total += labels.size(0)

correct += (predicted == labels).sum().item()


accuracy = correct / total

print(f"Test Accuracy: {accuracy * 100:.2f}%")

```
```

In this example, we start with a pre-trained ResNet18 model (`resnet`) and modify the final fully connected layer to suit our custom classification task. The model is then trained on the custom dataset. This approach harnesses the learned features from the original task (typically ImageNet classification) and adapts
```

them for the new dataset, demonstrating the efficiency of transfer learning.

This code structure can be adapted to various domains, such as medical imaging, object detection, or any task where transfer learning can provide a head start in model training. Adjustments can be made based on the specifics of the new task, including dataset size, class distribution, and the nature of the visual patterns to be learned.

- Pre-trained models are models that have already been trained on a large dataset, and can be used as a starting point for training a new CNN.

Pre-trained models can be fine-tuned for a specific task, such as recognizing handwritten digits. Transfer Learning: Efficient Wisdom Transfer in CNNs

Transfer learning is a potent technique in Convolutional Neural Networks (CNNs) that accelerates training efficiency by leveraging pre-trained models. It involves repurposing knowledge gained from one task to boost performance on a new, related task. This strategy is particularly valuable when labeled data for the target task is limited, as it allows the model to inherit valuable visual features from a broader dataset.

1. Why Transfer Learning?

- *Knowledge Transfer:* Pre-trained models capture generic visual features from large datasets, providing a knowledge foundation.

- *Efficiency:* Transfer learning minimizes the need for extensive training on a new task, saving time and computational resources.

2. Code Example: Transfer Learning with PyTorch and MobileNetV2

Let's employ PyTorch and a pre-trained MobileNetV2 model for transfer learning. The goal is to fine-tune the model on a custom dataset. Ensure PyTorch is installed (`pip install torch torchvision`).

```python
import torch
import torch.nn as nn
import torch.optim as optim
from torchvision import models, datasets, transforms
from torch.utils.data import DataLoader

# Step 1: Load the pre-trained MobileNetV2 model
```

```python
mobilenet = models.mobilenet_v2(pretrained=True)


# Step 2: Modify the final fully connected layer for
the new task
num_classes = 10  # Adjust based on your specific
task
mobilenet.classifier[1] =
nn.Linear(mobilenet.last_channel, num_classes)


# Step 3: Data preparation (assuming 'train_dataset'
and 'test_dataset' are loaded)
transform = transforms.Compose([
    transforms.Resize(256),
    transforms.CenterCrop(224),
    transforms.ToTensor(),
```

```python
    transforms.Normalize((0.5, 0.5, 0.5), (0.5, 0.5, 0.5))
])


# Assuming you have your custom dataset in the
'data' directory
train_dataset =
datasets.ImageFolder(root='data/train',
transform=transform)
test_dataset = datasets.ImageFolder(root='data/test',
transform=transform)


# Step 4: Create DataLoaders
train_loader = DataLoader(train_dataset,
batch_size=64, shuffle=True)
```

```
test_loader = DataLoader(test_dataset,
batch_size=64, shuffle=False)


# Step 5: Define loss function and optimizer
criterion = nn.CrossEntropyLoss()
optimizer = optim.SGD(mobilenet.parameters(),
lr=0.001, momentum=0.9)


# Step 6: Training
num_epochs = 5
for epoch in range(num_epochs):
    for inputs, labels in train_loader:
        optimizer.zero_grad()
        outputs = mobilenet(inputs)
        loss = criterion(outputs, labels)
```

```python
        loss.backward()

        optimizer.step()


# Step 7: Evaluation
correct = 0
total = 0
with torch.no_grad():
    for inputs, labels in test_loader:
        outputs = mobilenet(inputs)
        _, predicted = torch.max(outputs.data, 1)
        total += labels.size(0)
        correct += (predicted == labels).sum().item()


accuracy = correct / total
print(f"Test Accuracy: {accuracy * 100:.2f}%")
```

```

```

In this example, we start with a pre-trained MobileNetV2 model (`mobilenet`) and adapt it to a custom classification task by modifying the final fully connected layer. The model is then fine-tuned on the custom dataset, showcasing the efficiency and adaptability of transfer learning.

This code structure is versatile and applicable across diverse domains. Adjustments can be made based on the specifics of the new task, ensuring the model is tailored to capture relevant visual features efficiently.

Pre-trained models can be fine-tuned for a specific task, such as recognizing handwritten digits.

- Fine-tuning involves training only the last few layers of the CNN, while keeping the pre-trained weights for the earlier layers.

In summary, convolutional neural networks are a powerful tool for image classification tasks. Transfer learning and pre-trained models make it possible to train a CNN more efficiently, and to achieve higher accuracy on a new dataset. These techniques are essential for making

CNNs practical and scalable. With these tools, we can build intelligent systems that can recognize patterns and make predictions based on visual data.

CHAPTER 6: RECURRENT NEURAL NETWORKS (RNNs)

Welcome to the captivating realm of Recurrent Neural Networks (RNNs), where the power of sequential data handling unfolds. In this chapter, we dive into the intricacies of RNNs, exploring their unique ability to comprehend and analyze sequences of data, be it in natural language processing, time series analysis, or any domain where information unfolds over time.

Recurrent neural networks are one of the most powerful and popular types of neural networks. They're especially useful for processing sequential data, like text and speech. In this chapter, we'll learn about the basics of RNNs and how they work.

6.1 Sequential Data Handling: Unveiling the Time-Travelers of Neural Networks

Understanding Sequential Data:

Sequential data, by nature, possesses temporal dependencies. Whether it's the flow of words in a sentence, the evolution of stock prices, or the melody of a musical piece, the order of elements matters. RNNs are crafted to navigate this temporal landscape, making them formidable allies in tasks where context and order are paramount.

The Anatomy of RNNs:
At the core of an RNN lies a recurring loop that allows the network to maintain a hidden state, capturing information from previous steps. This hidden state becomes the key to preserving context across the sequence. As the network processes each element in the sequence, it adapts its hidden state, gradually assimilating a rich understanding of the data's temporal nuances.

Applications in Natural Language Processing:
In natural language processing, RNNs excel at understanding the nuance of language by considering the sequence of words. This makes

them potent tools for tasks like language modeling, sentiment analysis, and machine translation. The ability to grasp the context from preceding words allows RNNs to generate coherent and contextually relevant text.

Unleashing the Power in Time Series Analysis:

In the realm of time series analysis, RNNs become adept at forecasting future values based on historical patterns. Whether predicting stock prices, weather conditions, or energy consumption, RNNs harness the sequential nature of the data to make informed predictions.

Challenges and Solutions:

While RNNs offer a remarkable solution for sequential data, they are not without challenges. The vanishing gradient problem can hinder long-term dependencies, and the architecture requires careful tuning. Advanced variations like Long Short-Term Memory (LSTM) and Gated Recurrent Unit (GRU) have emerged to address these challenges, enhancing the ability of RNNs to capture intricate dependencies over extended sequences.

Embark on the RNN Journey:
As you venture into the exploration of Recurrent Neural Networks in this chapter, anticipate unraveling the mysteries of sequential data handling. Witness how RNNs unfold the layers of context in language, forecast the future in time series, and navigate the twists and turns of dynamic information. The journey promises to be both enlightening and empowering as we harness the

time-traveling capabilities of these neural networks.

Join the expedition into the heart of sequential data understanding with Recurrent Neural Networks.

RNNs are made up of repeating units called "cells." Each cell has a "memory" that remembers the previous inputs to the network. This allows the network to "remember" information over time, which is crucial for processing sequential data. The cells in an RNN are connected in a "recurrent" fashion, meaning that the output of one cell is fed back into the next cell. This allows the network to build up a "memory" of the inputs over time.

Next, let's talk about the "backpropagation through time" algorithm, which is used to train RNNs. This algorithm allows the network to learn from its mistakes and improve over time.

The "Backpropagation Through Time" (BPTT) algorithm is a variant of the standard backpropagation algorithm adapted for training Recurrent Neural Networks (RNNs). In BPTT, the gradients are calculated through time steps in a sequential manner, considering the dependencies introduced by the recurrent connections.

Let's walk through a simple code example of BPTT using PyTorch. In this example, we'll consider a basic RNN architecture and a simple sequence prediction task.

```python
import torch

import torch.nn as nn

import torch.optim as optim


# Define a simple RNN model

class SimpleRNN(nn.Module):

    def __init__(self, input_size, hidden_size,
output_size):

        super(SimpleRNN, self).__init__()
```

```python
        self.hidden_size = hidden_size
        self.rnn = nn.RNN(input_size, hidden_size,
batch_first=True)
        self.fc = nn.Linear(hidden_size, output_size)

    def forward(self, x):
        # RNN forward pass
        out, _ = self.rnn(x)

        # Use the last hidden state for prediction
        out = self.fc(out[:, -1, :])
        return out

# Create a simple dataset for sequence prediction
input_size = 1
```

```
hidden_size = 5

output_size = 1


# Generating a synthetic sequence dataset

sequence_length = 10

input_sequence = torch.randn((1, sequence_length,

input_size))

target_sequence = torch.randn((1, output_size))


# Instantiate the RNN model

rnn_model = SimpleRNN(input_size, hidden_size,

output_size)


# Define loss and optimizer

criterion = nn.MSELoss()
```

```python
optimizer = optim.SGD(rnn_model.parameters(),
lr=0.01)


# Training the RNN using BPTT
num_epochs = 100
for epoch in range(num_epochs):
    # Forward pass
    predictions = rnn_model(input_sequence)
    loss = criterion(predictions, target_sequence)

    # Backward pass through time
    optimizer.zero_grad()
    loss.backward()
    optimizer.step()
```

```
    if (epoch + 1) % 10 == 0:

        print(f'Epoch [{epoch + 1}/{num_epochs}], Loss:
{loss.item():.4f}')


# Testing the trained model
with torch.no_grad():
    test_input_sequence = torch.randn((1,
sequence_length, input_size))
    predicted_output =
rnn_model(test_input_sequence)
    print(f'Predicted Output:
{predicted_output.item()}')
```
```

**Explanation:**
```

1. Model Definition:

- We define a simple RNN model (`SimpleRNN`) with one RNN layer and a fully connected layer for sequence prediction.

2. Data Preparation:

- We generate a synthetic dataset with random input sequences and target sequences.

3. Training Loop:

- The model is trained using BPTT. The forward pass is executed, followed by the calculation of the loss. The backward pass through time (`loss.backward()`) ensures that gradients are calculated through the entire sequence.

4. Optimization:

- Gradients are used to update the model's parameters through the optimizer (`optimizer.step()`).

5. Testing:

- We test the trained model by providing a new input sequence and obtaining the predicted output.

This example provides a foundational understanding of how BPTT is applied in training an RNN. In practical scenarios, real-world sequential data would replace the synthetic data, and the model architecture and hyperparameters would be adjusted based on the specific task.

The backpropagation through time algorithm works by feeding the error back through the network, starting at the last cell and working backwards through the cells. This allows the network to adjust its weights and biases to reduce the error.

Now, let's talk about the "vanishing gradient problem" that can occur with RNNs. This is a problem where the gradient values become very small as they are propagated backwards through the network. As a result, the network can have trouble learning from its mistakes.

To solve the vanishing gradient problem, we can use a technique called "long short-term memory" (LSTM) networks. LSTM networks use a special type of cell that has a "gating mechanism" that helps to preserve the gradient values as they are propagated backwards through the network. This allows the network to learn more effectively from its mistakes.

6.2 Long Short-Term Memory (LSTM) Networks

Long Short-Term Memory (LSTM) networks are a specialized type of Recurrent Neural Networks (RNNs) designed to address the vanishing gradient problem and capture long-term dependencies in sequential data. LSTMs introduce memory cells, gates, and a more sophisticated architecture, enabling them to retain and selectively update information over extended sequences.

Key Components of LSTM:

1. Memory Cell:

- At the core of LSTM is a memory cell, a unit that stores information over time. This cell is equipped with mechanisms to add or remove information, allowing it to preserve relevant details.

2. Gates:

- LSTMs have three gates:

- *Forget Gate:* Decides what information from the cell state should be discarded.

- *Input Gate:* Determines what new information should be stored in the cell state.

- *Output Gate:* Filters information from the cell state to produce the output.

3. Cell State:

- The cell state acts as a conveyor belt, transporting relevant information across time steps.

LSTM in Action: A Code Example using PyTorch

Let's explore a simple example of an LSTM network using PyTorch. We'll use an LSTM for a sequence prediction task.

```python
import torch
import torch.nn as nn
import torch.optim as optim

# Define a simple LSTM model
class SimpleLSTM(nn.Module):
    def __init__(self, input_size, hidden_size, output_size):
        super(SimpleLSTM, self).__init__()
        self.hidden_size = hidden_size
        self.lstm = nn.LSTM(input_size, hidden_size, batch_first=True)
        self.fc = nn.Linear(hidden_size, output_size)
```

```python
def forward(self, x):
    # LSTM forward pass
    out, _ = self.lstm(x)

    # Use the last hidden state for prediction
    out = self.fc(out[:, -1, :])
    return out


# Create a simple dataset for sequence prediction
input_size = 1
hidden_size = 5
output_size = 1


# Generating a synthetic sequence dataset
sequence_length = 10
```

```python
input_sequence = torch.randn((1, sequence_length,
input_size))
target_sequence = torch.randn((1, output_size))


# Instantiate the LSTM model
lstm_model = SimpleLSTM(input_size, hidden_size,
output_size)


# Define loss and optimizer
criterion = nn.MSELoss()
optimizer = optim.SGD(lstm_model.parameters(),
lr=0.01)


# Training the LSTM
num_epochs = 100
```

```
for epoch in range(num_epochs):

    # Forward pass

    predictions = lstm_model(input_sequence)

    loss = criterion(predictions, target_sequence)


    # Backward pass

    optimizer.zero_grad()

    loss.backward()

    optimizer.step()


    if (epoch + 1) % 10 == 0:

        print(f'Epoch [{epoch + 1}/{num_epochs}], Loss:
{loss.item():.4f}')


# Testing the trained LSTM
```

```
with torch.no_grad():

    test_input_sequence = torch.randn((1,
sequence_length, input_size))

    predicted_output =
lstm_model(test_input_sequence)

    print(f'Predicted Output:
{predicted_output.item()}')

    ```
```

Explanation:

1. Model Definition:

- We define a simple LSTM model (`SimpleLSTM`) with one LSTM layer and a fully connected layer for sequence prediction.
```

2. Data Preparation:

- We generate a synthetic dataset with random input sequences and target sequences.

3. Training Loop:

- The model is trained using a similar process to the one in the previous example. The LSTM layer's architecture, with gates and memory cells, allows it to capture long-term dependencies.

4. Optimization:

- Gradients are used to update the model's parameters through the optimizer.

5. *Testing:*

- We test the trained LSTM by providing a new input sequence and obtaining the predicted output.

LSTMs are particularly effective in tasks where understanding long-range dependencies is crucial, such as language modeling, time series prediction, and speech recognition. Their architecture provides a solution to the challenges faced by traditional RNNs in capturing information over extended sequences.

CHAPTER 7: NATURAL LANGUAGE PROCESSING (NLP)

Welcome to the enthralling world of Natural Language Processing (NLP), where words become data and language transforms into a playground for intelligent machines. In this chapter, we delve into the foundational concept of Text Representation, a pivotal step in empowering machines to understand and process human language.

7.1 Text Representation: The Art of Translating Words into Numbers

Why Text Representation Matters:

- In the digital realm, machines don't comprehend words the way humans do. Text representation bridges this gap by converting textual information into numerical form, enabling machines to navigate the linguistic landscape.

The Challenge of Raw Text:

- Raw text is an intricate web of words, syntax, and semantics. To make sense of it, we need to transform it into a format machines can digest. Text representation provides the key to unlocking the insights hidden in language.

One-Hot Encoding:

- A rudimentary yet fundamental method, one-hot encoding assigns a unique index to each word in a vocabulary. Each word is represented as a vector where all elements are zero except the one corresponding to its index. While simple, it lacks the ability to capture relationships between words.

Here's a code example demonstrating One-Hot Encoding using PyTorch:

```python
```

```python
import torch

import torch.nn.functional as F


# Sample sentence

sentence = "NLP is fascinating!"


# Tokenizing the sentence into words

words = sentence.split()


# Creating a vocabulary

vocabulary = set(words)


# One-Hot Encoding Function using PyTorch

def one_hot_encode(word, vocab):

    index = vocab.index(word)
```

```python
    encoding = F.one_hot(torch.tensor(index),
len(vocab))

    return encoding


# One-Hot Encode Each Word
one_hot_encoded_words = [one_hot_encode(word,
list(vocabulary)) for word in words]


# Displaying the Results
for word, encoding in zip(words,
one_hot_encoded_words):
    print(f'{word}: {encoding.numpy()}')
```

Explanation:

1. Sample Sentence and Tokenization:

- Same as before, we start with a sample sentence and tokenize it into individual words.

2. Creating a Vocabulary:

- A vocabulary is formed by collecting unique words from the tokenized sentence.

3. One-Hot Encoding Function using PyTorch:

- The `one_hot_encode` function takes a word and the vocabulary as input and returns a

one-hot encoded tensor using PyTorch's
`F.one_hot` function.

4. One-Hot Encode Each Word:

- For each word in the sentence, we use the PyTorch one-hot encoding function to generate its numerical representation.

5. Displaying the Results:

- The final step involves displaying the one-hot encoded tensors for each word in the sentence.

This PyTorch example achieves the same result as the previous one but leverages PyTorch's functionality for one-hot encoding.

Word Embeddings:

- Enter word embeddings, a more sophisticated approach. Words are mapped to dense vectors in a continuous vector space. This method captures semantic relationships, allowing similar words to be closer in this space. Popular embeddings like Word2Vec and GloVe have revolutionized NLP tasks.

Word embeddings are a more advanced technique compared to one-hot encoding. In this example, I'll demonstrate using pre-trained word embeddings with PyTorch's `torch.nn.Embedding` module. We'll use the popular GloVe embeddings.

```python
import torch
import torch.nn as nn
from torch.nn.functional import embedding


# Sample sentence
sentence = "NLP is fascinating!"


# Tokenizing the sentence into words
words = sentence.split()
```

```python
# Pre-trained GloVe word embeddings
(50-dimensional for simplicity)
glove_embeddings = {
    'NLP': torch.tensor([0.1, 0.2, 0.3, 0.4, 0.5]),
    'is': torch.tensor([0.2, 0.3, 0.4, 0.5, 0.6]),
    'fascinating!': torch.tensor([0.3, 0.4, 0.5, 0.6, 0.7]),
}


# Word Embeddings Function
def word_embedding(word, embeddings):
    return embeddings[word]


# Word Embed Each Word
```

```
word_embeddings = [word_embedding(word,
glove_embeddings) for word in words]

# Displaying the Results
for word, embedding_vector in zip(words,
word_embeddings):
  print(f'{word}: {embedding_vector.numpy()}')
```

Explanation:

1. Sample Sentence and Tokenization:

- The sample sentence is tokenized into individual words.

2. Pre-trained GloVe Word Embeddings:

- For simplicity, I've manually created a small set of GloVe-like embeddings. In real scenarios, you would use pre-trained embeddings like those available from GloVe or Word2Vec.

3. Word Embeddings Function:

- The `word_embedding` function takes a word and a dictionary of pre-trained embeddings and returns the embedding vector for that word.

4. *Word Embed Each Word:*

- For each word in the sentence, we use the word embeddings function to obtain its embedding vector.

5. *Displaying the Results:*

- The final step involves displaying the word embeddings for each word in the sentence.

In practice, you would typically use pre-trained embeddings for a broader vocabulary and embedding dimensionality.

The Power of Word2Vec:

- Word2Vec represents words as vectors by predicting the context in which words appear. This method imbues words with meaning based on their usage context, facilitating a deeper understanding of semantics.

Creating Word2Vec embeddings involves training a model on a large corpus, and it might be impractical to train it within this chat. However, I can guide you on how to use pre-trained Word2Vec embeddings. We'll use the popular `gensim` library for this example.

First, make sure to install the library:

```bash
```

```
pip install gensim
```

```
```

Now, you can use the following code to load pre-trained Word2Vec embeddings and apply them to your sample sentence:

```python
import gensim.downloader as api

# Download pre-trained Word2Vec model (large model, might take some time)
w2v_model = api.load('word2vec-google-news-300')

# Sample sentence
```

```python
sentence = "NLP is fascinating!"


# Tokenizing the sentence into words
words = sentence.split()


# Word2Vec Embedding Function
def word2vec_embedding(word, model):
    try:
        return model[word]
    except KeyError:
        # Handle out-of-vocabulary words
        return [0.0] * model.vector_size


# Word2Vec Embed Each Word
```

```
word2vec_embeddings =
[word2vec_embedding(word, w2v_model) for word
in words]

# Displaying the Results
for word, embedding_vector in zip(words,
word2vec_embeddings):
    print(f'{word}: {embedding_vector}')
```

This code uses the Word2Vec embeddings from the Google News dataset. The `word2vec_embedding` function fetches the embedding for each word. Note that this is a large model, so downloading might take some time. If you have a smaller corpus, consider using a smaller pre-trained Word2Vec model.

GloVe: Global Vectors for Word Representation:

- GloVe, on the other hand, leverages global word co-occurrence statistics to generate word embeddings. It excels in capturing global relationships and has become a cornerstone in various NLP applications.

We'll use the GloVe embeddings available through the `torchtext` library. First, make sure to install the library:

```bash
```

pip install torchtext

` ` `

Now, you can use the following code to load pre-trained GloVe embeddings and apply them to your sample sentence:

```python
import torch
from torchtext.vocab import GloVe
from nltk.tokenize import word_tokenize
import nltk
nltk.download('punkt')    # Download the punkt
tokenizer
```

```python
# Sample sentence
sentence = "NLP is fascinating!"


# Tokenizing the sentence into words
words = word_tokenize(sentence)


# Load pre-trained GloVe embeddings
(50-dimensional for simplicity)
glove = GloVe(name='6B', dim=50)


# GloVe Embedding Function
def glove_embedding(word, embeddings):
    try:
        return embeddings[word].numpy()
    except KeyError:
```

```
# Handle out-of-vocabulary words
return [0.0] * embeddings.vectors.shape[1]


# GloVe Embed Each Word
glove_embeddings = [glove_embedding(word, glove)
for word in words]


# Displaying the Results
for word, embedding_vector in zip(words,
glove_embeddings):
    print(f'{word}: {embedding_vector}')
```

This code uses the 50-dimensional GloVe embeddings from the 6B version available in `torchtext`. The `glove_embedding` function fetches the embedding for each word. If you need a different dimensionality, you can choose from other available GloVe versions (e.g., `name='840B'` for 300-dimensional embeddings).

The Emergence of Transformer-Based Models:

- Recent advancements have witnessed the rise of transformer-based models like BERT and GPT, which capture contextual information at an unparalleled level. These models redefine the landscape of text representation with their attention mechanisms.

As we embark on the exploration of Text Representation in NLP, anticipate unraveling the threads that weave words into meaning. From the simplicity of one-hot encoding to the intricacies of transformer-based models, each technique brings us closer to the goal of enabling machines to comprehend and generate human-like language.

Join the expedition into the heart of NLP with Text Representation. The journey promises not only to demystify the mechanisms behind language understanding but also to empower you with the knowledge to craft intelligent systems that navigate the rich tapestry of human expression.

7.2 Sequence-to-Sequence Models

Sequence-to-sequence models are another type of NLP model that we can use for tasks like machine translation. These models take a sequence of text as input and generate a new sequence of text as output. They are really good at capturing the relationships between words and sentences.

Sequence-to-sequence models use a special type of neural network called a "recurrent neural network" (RNN) to process the input sequence. The RNN keeps track of the previous words in the input sequence and uses that information to generate the next word in the output sequence. This allows the model to learn the relationships between words and sentences.

Here's a simple example of a sequence-to-sequence model using PyTorch and the popular `torch.nn` module:

```python
import torch
import torch.nn as nn
import torch.optim as optim
```

```python
# Define the Seq2Seq Model
class Seq2Seq(nn.Module):
    def __init__(self, input_dim, hidden_dim,
output_dim):
        super(Seq2Seq, self).__init__()

        # Encoder RNN
        self.encoder = nn.RNN(input_dim, hidden_dim)

        # Decoder RNN
        self.decoder = nn.RNN(hidden_dim,
hidden_dim)

        # Fully connected layer for output
```

```python
    self.fc_out = nn.Linear(hidden_dim,
output_dim)


    def forward(self, src, trg):
        # src: source sequence
        # trg: target sequence


        # Encoder forward pass
        enc_output, enc_hidden = self.encoder(src)


        # Decoder forward pass
        dec_output, _ = self.decoder(trg, enc_hidden)


        # Output layer
        output = self.fc_out(dec_output)
```

```python
    return output


# Define input and output dimensions
input_dim = 10  # Dimensionality of input sequence
hidden_dim = 20  # Dimensionality of hidden states
output_dim = 10  # Dimensionality of output
sequence


# Instantiate the Seq2Seq model
seq2seq_model = Seq2Seq(input_dim, hidden_dim,
output_dim)


# Define loss function and optimizer
criterion = nn.MSELoss()
```

```python
optimizer = optim.Adam(seq2seq_model.parameters(), lr=0.001)

# Dummy input sequences
src_sequence = torch.randn((5, 3, input_dim))  # (sequence_length, batch_size, input_dim)
trg_sequence = torch.randn((5, 3, hidden_dim))  # (sequence_length, batch_size, hidden_dim)

# Training loop
num_epochs = 100
for epoch in range(num_epochs):
    # Forward pass
    output_sequence = seq2seq_model(src_sequence, trg_sequence)
```

```
# Compute the loss

loss = criterion(output_sequence, trg_sequence)


# Backward pass and optimization

optimizer.zero_grad()

loss.backward()

optimizer.step()


# Print the loss

print(f'Epoch [{epoch + 1}/{num_epochs}], Loss:
{loss.item():.4f}')

```
```
```

Explanation:

1. Seq2Seq Model Architecture:

- The `Seq2Seq` class defines a simple sequence-to-sequence model with an encoder RNN, a decoder RNN, and a fully connected layer for output.

2. Forward Pass:

- In the `forward` method, the input sequence (`src`) is passed through the encoder, and the hidden state is then used as the initial hidden state for the decoder. The decoder's output is passed through a fully connected layer to obtain the final output.

3. Loss Calculation:

- The mean squared error loss is used to calculate the difference between the predicted output and the target output.

4. Training Loop:

- The model is trained using a dummy input sequence (`src_sequence`) and target sequence (`trg_sequence`). The model parameters are updated through backpropagation.

This example provides a foundational understanding of a sequence-to-sequence model. In real-world scenarios, you would use more complex architectures, larger datasets, and fine-tune hyperparameters based on the specific task.

CHAPTER 8: COMPUTER VISION APPLICATIONS

Moving on to computer vision! Computer vision is a field of AI that uses machine learning to analyze and understand images. There are many different applications of computer vision, such as object detection, image classification, and image segmentation. Let's start by talking about object detection.

8.1 Object Detection

Object detection is a task where we want to identify the objects in an image and where they are located. For example, we might want to detect cars, people, and traffic signs in a street scene. This is a challenging task because objects can vary greatly in appearance and location. But, we can use neural networks to learn the features of different objects and to detect them in images.

It's no problem at all! So, one of the most popular algorithms for object detection is called "YOLO" (You Only Look Once). YOLO uses a convolutional neural network (CNN) to detect objects in images. CNNs are especially good at learning the features of objects, such as their shape and color.

YOLO works by dividing an image into a grid and then predicting the location and category of each object in the image. It does this by looking at the image once and then making its predictions. This is what "You Only Look Once" means. The predictions are then refined using a technique called "non-maximum suppression." This allows the model to only keep the most confident predictions. This approach allows YOLO to detect objects quickly and accurately. It is very popular for tasks like autonomous driving, where real-time object detection is important.

Let's talk about image classification. This is a task where we want to classify an image into one or more categories. For example, we might want to classify an image as a cat or a dog. To do this, we can use a special type of neural network called a "convolutional neural network" (CNN). CNNs have become the standard for image classification, thanks to their ability to learn the features of images.

Implementing YOLO (You Only Look Once) from scratch is quite involved due to its complex architecture and training requirements. It's typically trained on large datasets, and the model architecture involves convolutional neural networks.

Here, I'll provide a simplified example using a pre-trained YOLO model from the `torchvision` library. Make sure to install the library first:

```bash
pip install torchvision
```

Now, you can use the following code:

```python
import torch
from torchvision import transforms
from torchvision.models.detection import yolov3
from PIL import Image, ImageDraw
import requests
```

```
# Load pre-trained YOLO model

model = yolov3(pretrained=True)


# Set the model to evaluation mode

model.eval()


# Load and preprocess an image

image_url                                    =

"https://raw.githubusercontent.com/pytorch/vision/

main/references/detection/data/ski.jpg"

image     =     Image.open(requests.get(image_url,

stream=True).raw).convert("RGB")


# Preprocess the image
```

```python
transform = transforms.Compose([
    transforms.ToTensor(),
        transforms.Resize((416, 416)),   # YOLO model
input size
])
input_image = transform(image).unsqueeze(0)


# Make predictions
with torch.no_grad():
    predictions = model(input_image)


# Visualize the predictions on the image
draw = ImageDraw.Draw(image)
for prediction in predictions[0]["boxes"]:
```

```
draw.rectangle(prediction.tolist(), outline="red",
width=2)


# Display the image with bounding boxes
image.show()
```
```

## Explanation:

### 1. Load Pre-trained YOLO Model:

- We use the `yolov3` function from `torchvision.models.detection` to load a pre-trained YOLOv3 model.

### 2. Set the Model to Evaluation Mode:
```

- The model is set to evaluation mode using `model.eval()`.

3. *Load and Preprocess Image:*

- We load an example image from the web, convert it to RGB, and apply necessary transformations to match the YOLO model input size.

4. *Make Predictions*:

- We pass the preprocessed image through the YOLO model to obtain predictions. The predictions include bounding boxes, class labels, and confidence scores.

5. *Visualize Predictions*:

- Using `ImageDraw`, we draw bounding boxes on the original image based on the predictions.

6. *Display the Image*:

- The final image with bounding boxes is displayed.

Note: This example uses a pre-trained model for simplicity. In a real-world scenario, you would typically fine-tune the model on a specific dataset for your object detection task. Also, this is a basic example, and the actual implementation of YOLO involves more details such as non-maximum suppression for handling overlapping bounding boxes and post-processing steps. If you need a more customized solution, consider using a dedicated object detection library or framework.

8.2 Image Generation with Generative Adversarial Networks (GANs):

Generative Adversarial Networks (GANs) are a special type of neural network that can generate new images that look similar to real images. GANs consist of two neural networks: a generator and a discriminator. The generator generates new images, while the discriminator tries to distinguish between real and generated images.

The generator and discriminator work together in a competitive way. The discriminator tries to get better at distinguishing real and generated images, while the generator tries to get better at fooling the discriminator. This competition between the two networks helps to improve the quality of the generated images. GANs have been used to generate realistic images of human faces, animals, and even works of art.

GANs consist of a generator and a discriminator network, and they are trained simultaneously through a competitive process. Here, I'll provide a simple example using PyTorch to create a GAN for generating images.

Make sure to install PyTorch first:

```bash
pip install torch
```

Now, let's dive into a basic GAN example:

```python
import torch
import torch.nn as nn
import torch.optim as optim
from torchvision import datasets, transforms
from torch.utils.data import DataLoader
import matplotlib.pyplot as plt


# Set random seed for reproducibility
torch.manual_seed(42)


# Define the generator and discriminator networks
class Generator(nn.Module):
    def __init__(self, latent_dim, output_dim):
        super(Generator, self).__init__()
```

```python
        self.main = nn.Sequential(

            nn.Linear(latent_dim, 128),

            nn.ReLU(),

            nn.Linear(128, output_dim),

            nn.Tanh()  # Output in the range [-1, 1] for
images
            )


    def forward(self, z):

        return self.main(z)



class Discriminator(nn.Module):

    def __init__(self, input_dim):

        super(Discriminator, self).__init__()
```

```python
        self.main = nn.Sequential(

            nn.Linear(input_dim, 128),

            nn.LeakyReLU(0.2),

            nn.Linear(128, 1),

            nn.Sigmoid()  # Output a probability between
0 and 1

        )


    def forward(self, x):

        return self.main(x)



# Set parameters

latent_dim = 100

output_dim = 784  # 28x28 for MNIST images
```

```python
batch_size = 64

lr = 0.0002

epochs = 20


# Create generator and discriminator instances

generator = Generator(latent_dim, output_dim)

discriminator = Discriminator(output_dim)


# Define loss function and optimizers

criterion = nn.BCELoss()  # Binary Cross Entropy
Loss

optimizer_g = optim.Adam(generator.parameters(),
lr=lr)

optimizer_d =
optim.Adam(discriminator.parameters(), lr=lr)
```

```python
# Load MNIST dataset
transform = transforms.Compose([
    transforms.ToTensor(),
    transforms.Normalize((0.5,), (0.5,)),
])

train_dataset = datasets.MNIST(root='./data',
train=True, download=True, transform=transform)
dataloader = DataLoader(train_dataset,
batch_size=batch_size, shuffle=True,
drop_last=True)

# Training loop
for epoch in range(epochs):
```

```
for real_images, _ in dataloader:

    batch_size_curr = real_images.size(0)


    # Train Discriminator

    discriminator.zero_grad()

    real_labels = torch.ones(batch_size_curr, 1)

    fake_labels = torch.zeros(batch_size_curr, 1)


    # Real images

    output_real =

discriminator(real_images.view(-1, output_dim))

    loss_real = criterion(output_real, real_labels)


    # Generate fake images
```

```
noise = torch.randn(batch_size_curr,
latent_dim)
fake_images = generator(noise)
output_fake =
discriminator(fake_images.detach())
loss_fake = criterion(output_fake, fake_labels)

# Backpropagation and optimization
loss_d = loss_real + loss_fake
loss_d.backward()
optimizer_d.step()

# Train Generator
generator.zero_grad()
output_gen = discriminator(fake_images)
```

```python
    loss_g = criterion(output_gen, real_labels)

    # Backpropagation and optimization
    loss_g.backward()
    optimizer_g.step()

    # Print progress
    print(f'Epoch [{epoch + 1}/{epochs}], Loss D: {loss_d.item():.4f}, Loss G: {loss_g.item():.4f}')

# Generate and visualize some fake images
with torch.no_grad():
    test_noise = torch.randn(16, latent_dim)
    generated_images = generator(test_noise).view(-1, 28, 28).numpy()
```

```
plt.figure(figsize=(8, 8))

for i in range(16):

    plt.subplot(4, 4, i + 1)

    plt.imshow(generated_images[i], cmap='gray')

    plt.axis('off')

plt.show()
```
```

**Explanation:**

*1. Generator and Discriminator Networks:*

- We define a simple generator and discriminator neural network architecture using fully connected layers.
```

2. Loss Function and Optimizers:

- We use Binary Cross Entropy Loss (`nn.BCELoss`) for both generator and discriminator. Two separate optimizers are defined for updating the parameters of each network.

3. MNIST Dataset:

- We use the MNIST dataset for training. The images are normalized and transformed to tensors.

4. Training Loop:

- The training loop consists of alternating updates between the discriminator and generator. The discriminator aims to distinguish between real and fake images, while the generator aims to generate images that fool the discriminator.

5. Visualization:

- After training, we generate and visualize some fake images produced by the generator.

Note: This is a simplified example, and GANs can be more complex in practice. Further adjustments and considerations, such as different architectures, hyperparameter tuning, and regularization techniques, may be needed for specific tasks and datasets.

In summary, GANs are a powerful and exciting new technology for generating realistic images. They have a wide range of applications, from generating art to improving medical imaging. As the technology develops, GANs are likely to have an even greater impact on our lives. This is just the beginning of what is sure to be an exciting journey into the world of GANs!

CHAPTER 9: MODEL DEPLOYMENT

Model deployment is the process of putting a trained machine learning model into production, so that it can be used in the real world. This is usually done to put the model's predictions into action, such as making decisions or classifying data. Model deployment is important because it allows organizations to make use of their machine learning models in a practical way. It's like taking the model out of the lab and putting it to work in the real world.

9.1 Exporting Models

The first step in deploying a machine learning model is to export it from the development environment. This means packaging the model in a way that makes it easy to use in the real world.

Now, let's talk about some common formats for model export. The most common formats are PyTorch SavedModel and ONNX. PyTorch SavedModel is a format developed by Google that is specific to the PyTorch library. ONNX, or Open Neural Network Exchange, is a more general format that can be used with many different machine learning libraries.

With PyTorch SavedModel, the model is represented as a graph of PyTorch operations. This graph can then be saved in a file that can be loaded by other PyTorch applications. PyTorch SavedModel also supports things like model checkpoints, which allow you to save the model in stages during training. That way, you can restore the model to a specific point in the training process.

Now, let's talk about how to export a model to PyTorch SavedModel. First, you need to have a trained model in TensorFlow. Then, you can use the "saver" module to create a SavedModel file. This file can then be used by other PyTorch applications. The cool thing about PyTorch

SavedModel is that it's not just for TensorFlow. There are tools that allow you to convert a PyTorch SavedModel into other formats, like ONNX. This makes it easy to use your model with different machine learning libraries.

Now, let's talk about how to load a SavedModel and use it to make predictions. First, you need to import the SavedModel file into your code. Then, you can use the "load" function to load the model. Once the model is loaded, you can use it to make predictions by passing data to the "predict" function.

Let's create a simple example in Python using PyTorch to illustrate the process of loading a SavedModel and making predictions. In this example, I'll assume you have a SavedModel directory named "my_saved_model" with a model that takes a single input and produces a single output.

```python
import PyTorch as tf
import numpy as np


# Define a sample input data for prediction
sample_input = np.array([[1.0, 2.0, 3.0]],
dtype=np.float32)


# Load the SavedModel
saved_model_path = 'my_saved_model'
```

```
loaded_model =
tf.saved_model.load(saved_model_path)


# Use the loaded model to make predictions
prediction                                    =
loaded_model.predict(tf.constant(sample_input))


# Print the prediction
print("Prediction:", prediction.numpy())
```
```

**Explanation:**


**1. Import torch::**
```

- We import the PyTorch library to work with SavedModels.

2. *Define Sample Input Data*:

- We create a sample input data array for making predictions. In this case, it's a 2D NumPy array with a single row.

3. *Load the SavedModel:*

- We use the `tf.saved_model.load` function to load the SavedModel located at the specified path ("my_saved_model").

4. Make Predictions:

- The loaded model has a `predict` function that we can use to make predictions. We pass the sample input data to this function, and it returns the prediction.

5. Print Prediction:

- Finally, we print the prediction obtained from the model.

Keep in mind that the actual code structure may vary based on the specifics of your SavedModel and the requirements of your model's input and output. It's important to adapt the code to match the structure and features of your particular model.

9.2 Integrating Models into Applications

Integrating models into applications is a key part of putting machine learning into production. There are a few different ways to do this, but we'll focus on using a REST API. This allows you to expose the model's functionality through a simple API, which can be accessed from any programming language. First, you need to set up a web server that will host your API. For this, we'll use a library called Flask. Flask is a simple web framework for

Python that makes it easy to create web applications. Once you have Flask installed, you can create a simple API for your model.

To create the API, you need to create a function that takes in some input data and returns the model's predictions. This function will be exposed as the API endpoint. In this function, you'll need to load the model and make the predictions. Once the function is created, you can use Flask to create a web application that exposes the function as an API endpoint.

Let's create a simple example using Flask to create a web API that exposes a machine learning model's predictions. For simplicity, I'll assume a dummy model and input data.

```python
from flask import Flask, request, jsonify
import PyTorch as tf
import numpy as np


# Create a Flask web application
app = Flask(__name__)


# Load the SavedModel
saved_model_path = 'my_saved_model'
loaded_model =
tf.saved_model.load(saved_model_path)
```

```python
# Define the API endpoint function
@app.route('/predict', methods=['POST'])
def predict():
    # Get input data from the request
    input_data = request.json['data']

    # Ensure the input data is in the correct format
    (adjust based on your model's requirements)
    input_data = np.array(input_data,
dtype=np.float32)

    # Make predictions using the loaded model
    prediction =
loaded_model.predict(tf.constant([input_data]))
```

```
# Return the predictions as JSON

return jsonify({'prediction':

prediction.numpy().tolist()})


# Run the Flask application

if __name__ == '__main__':

    app.run(debug=True)

```

Explanation:

1. Import Flask and TensorFlow: - We import Flask to create a web application and PyTorch to work with the SavedModel and make predictions.

2. Create Flask Application:

  - We create a Flask web application using `Flask(__name__)`.

3. Load the SavedModel:

  - We load the SavedModel (located at "my_saved_model") using `tf.saved_model.load`.

4. Define API Endpoint Function:

  - We define a function (`predict`) that will be exposed as the API endpoint ("/predict"). This function takes input data from the request, processes it, makes predictions using the loaded model, and returns the predictions as JSON.

5. Run Flask Application:

- We run the Flask application using `app.run(debug=True)`. This starts a local development server.

6. Making API Requests:

- To make predictions, you can send a POST request to the "/predict" endpoint with input data in the request body as JSON. Adjust the input data format based on your model's requirements.

Remember that this is a basic example, and in a real-world scenario, you would need to handle more aspects, such as error checking, security considerations, and potentially deploying the application to a production server. Adjust the code based on your specific model and API requirements.

Now, let's talk about how to use this API. To use the API, you'll need to send some data to the API endpoint in the correct format. Once you've sent the data, the API will return the predictions. You can then use this data in your application however you want.

CHAPTER 10: PERFORMANCE OPTIMIZATION

10.1 Hardware Acceleration

Hardware acceleration is a key part of performance optimization. This involves using specialized hardware like GPUs and TPUs to speed up the training and inference of machine learning models. Hardware acceleration takes advantage of the parallel processing capabilities of GPUs and TPUs. These chips have many cores that can work on different parts of the data at the same time. This allows them to train and infer models much faster than traditional CPUs. It's like having many people working on a problem at the same time instead of just one person.

Let's talk about how hardware acceleration is used in practice. TPyTorchhere are two main ways to use hardware acceleration:

1. with GPUs:

PyTorch with GPUs is one of the most popular ways to accelerate machine learning. It uses NVIDIA GPUs to train and infer models much faster than with traditional CPUs. This can be done on both local machines and cloud services like Google Cloud Platform and Amazon Web Services. The first thing you need to use PyTorch with GPUs is a compatible GPU. NVIDIA GPUs are the most popular option, and there are different options to choose from based on your needs. Once you have a GPU, you can install the CUDA toolkit and PyTorch with GPU support.

To use PyTorch with GPUs, you need to initialize a PyTorch session with the flag "gpu=True". This tells PyTorch to use the GPU instead of the CPU for training and inference. You can also specify the specific GPU you want to use with the "device" flag.

Here's an example code snippet that showcases using a specific GPU with TensorFlow:

```python
import PyTorch as tf

# Check if GPU is available
if tf.test.gpu_device_name():
    print('Default GPU Device:
{}'.format(tf.test.gpu_device_name()))
else:
    print("No GPU available. PyTorch will use CPU.")
```

```
# Specify GPU device

gpu_device = '/gpu:0'  # You can change the index
(e.g., '/gpu:1') based on your setup


# Create a PyTorch session with the specified GPU
device
with tf.device(gpu_device):
    # Your PyTorch code here
    # ...


# Alternatively, you can use the following to specify
GPU during session creation
# config = tf.ConfigProto(device_count={'GPU': 1})
# Specify the number of GPUs
# session = tf.Session(config=config)
```

```
` ` `
```

Explanation:

1. Check GPU Availability:

  - The code checks if a GPU is available using `tf.test.gpu_device_name()`.

2. Specify GPU Device:

  - You can specify the GPU device using the "device" flag (e.g., '/gpu:0'). Change the index based on the GPU you want to use.

3. Create PyTorch Session with GPU:

- The code creates a PyTorch session with the specified GPU device. Any subsequent PyTorch operations within this session will use the specified GPU.

4. *Alternative Approach*:

- An alternative approach is to use `tf.ConfigProto` during session creation to specify the number of GPUs. Uncomment the relevant lines in the code if you want to use this approach.

Explicitly specifying GPU usage may not be necessary in most cases, but you have the flexibility to control it based on your requirements.

2. PyTorch with TPUs

The next is PyTorch with TPUs. TPUs, or Tensor Processing Units, are specialized hardware designed specifically for TensorFlow. They are much faster than GPUs and are available on Google Cloud Platform PyTorch with TPUs works in a similar way to PyTorch with GPUs, but with a few key differences. First, we need to initialize the PyTorch session with the "tpu=True" flag. Second, we need to specify the TPU device with the "tpu_cores" flag.

It's important to note that PyTorch with TPUs (Tensor Processing Units) usually involves using the Google Colab environment, as TPUs are specific hardware accelerators provided by Google. Below is an example illustrating how you can use TPUs in PyTorch within a Colab notebook.

```python
import PyTorch as tf
import os

# Check if TPU is available in the Colab
environment
if 'COLAB_TPU_ADDR' not in os.environ:
```

```
    raise RuntimeError("TPU not found. Make sure
you are running this code in a Google Colab
notebook.")

# Connect to the TPU
tpu_address = 'grpc://' +
os.environ['COLAB_TPU_ADDR']
tpu_cluster_resolver =
tf.distribute.cluster_resolver.TPUClusterResolver(tpu
=tpu_address)
tf.config.experimental_connect_to_cluster(tpu_clust
er_resolver)
tf.tpu.experimental.initialize_tpu_system(tpu_cluste
r_resolver)
```

```python
# Create a strategy for distributing training on the
TPU
tpu_strategy =
tf.distribute.experimental.TPUStrategy(tpu_cluster_
resolver)

# Within the strategy scope, define and compile
your model
with tpu_strategy.scope():
    # Define and compile your PyTorch model here
    model = tf.keras.Sequential([
        # Your model layers here
    ])
```

```
    model.compile(optimizer='adam',

loss='sparse_categorical_crossentropy',

metrics=['accuracy'])


# Train the model using the TPU strategy

# Note: You should use TPU-compatible datasets

for optimal performance

# Example: model.fit(train_dataset, epochs=5,

steps_per_epoch=100)

```
```

Explanation:

1. Check TPU Availability in Colab:
```

- The code checks if the Colab environment has access to a TPU by verifying the presence of the "COLAB_TPU_ADDR" environment variable.

2. Connect to TPU:

- It connects to the TPU using the TPUClusterResolver and initializes the TPU system.

3. Create TPU Strategy:

- It creates a TPU strategy for distributing training on the TPU using `tf.distribute.experimental.TPUStrategy`.

4. Model Definition within TPU Strategy:

- Inside the TPU strategy scope, you define and compile your PyTorch model. The TPU strategy ensures that operations are distributed across the TPU cores.

5. Train the Model:

- Train the model using TPU-compatible datasets for optimal performance. Ensure that your dataset and input pipeline are compatible with TPUs for efficient training.

Note: The TPU strategy is essential for using TPUs effectively in distributed training. The provided example assumes a simplified model definition, and you should replace it with your actual model architecture and training setup. Additionally, adapt the training loop based on your dataset and training requirements.

- 10.2 Quantization and Pruning

Quantization and pruning are powerful techniques in the realm of neural network optimization, aiming to reduce model size and computational complexity without compromising performance. Let's delve into each technique:

Quantization:

Quantization involves reducing the precision of numerical representations in a model, typically from 32-bit floating-point numbers to lower bit-widths like 8-bit integers. This process minimizes memory requirements and accelerates inference on hardware like CPUs and GPUs.

Why Quantize?

1. Memory Efficiency: Lower bit-widths require less memory, crucial for deployment on resource-constrained devices.

2. Faster Inference: Quantized models often exhibit faster inference times due to reduced data movement and storage.

Implementation:

In PyTorch, quantization can be achieved using the `torch.quantization` module. This involves converting a pre-trained model to a quantized version, considering both weights and activations.

```python
```

```
import torch

from torch.quantization import quantize_dynamic


# Load your pre-trained model

model = ...


# Quantize the model dynamically

quantized_model = quantize_dynamic(model,

{torch.nn.Linear}, dtype=torch.qint8)

```
```

Pruning:

Pruning involves removing certain connections (weights or neurons) from a neural network, essentially creating a sparse model. Pruned
```

models retain high accuracy while benefiting from reduced model size and computational requirements.

Why Prune?

1. Model Compression: Sparse models consume less memory and disk space.

2. Faster Inference: Fewer computations lead to faster inference.

3. Energy Efficiency: Pruned models may be more energy-efficient, crucial for edge devices.

Implementation:

In PyTorch, pruning is facilitated by the `torch.nn.utils.prune` module. This module allows you to apply pruning techniques to specific layers or connections.

```python
import torch
from torch.nn.utils import prune

# Load your pre-trained model
model = ...

# Specify pruning parameters and prune the model
pruning_params = {'name': 'weight', 'amount': 0.2}
prune.l1_unstructured(model.conv1,
pruning_params)
```

Considerations:

1. Fine-Tuning: After quantization or pruning, it's often beneficial to fine-tune the model to regain some lost accuracy.

2. Evaluation Metrics: Assess the trade-off between model size, inference speed, and accuracy based on your application's requirements.

Incorporating quantization and pruning in your PyTorch workflow can lead to more efficient models, especially in scenarios where resource constraints are a primary concern. Experiment

with different configurations to find the right
balance for your specific use case.

CHAPTER 11: PYTORCH ECOSYSTEM AND COMMUNITY

In the vast and dynamic landscape of PyTorch, the ecosystem and community play pivotal roles in empowering developers and researchers. Let's explore the rich offerings in terms of libraries and frameworks that make PyTorch an expansive and vibrant environment.

11.1 Libraries and Frameworks:

a. TorchVision: Enhancing Vision Tasks

TorchVision is a library that extends PyTorch for computer vision tasks. It provides utilities for image and video processing, pre-trained models, and dataset handling. Whether you're working on image classification or object detection, TorchVision simplifies the development process.

```python
import torchvision.transforms as transforms
from torchvision import models

# Example: Using a pre-trained ResNet model for image classification
```

```python
model = models.resnet50(pretrained=True)
```

b. TorchText: NLP Made Easier

For natural language processing (NLP) tasks, TorchText is a go-to library. It streamlines text data preprocessing, tokenization, and provides access to popular datasets. It facilitates the development of robust models for sentiment analysis, language translation, and more.

```python
import torchtext
from torchtext.data import Field, BucketIterator
```

```
# Example: Loading a sentiment analysis dataset
TEXT = Field(tokenize='spacy',
include_lengths=True)
LABEL = Field(dtype=torch.float)
train_data, test_data =
torchtext.datasets.IMDB.splits(TEXT, LABEL)
```

c. TorchAudio: Sound Processing Excellence

TorchAudio extends PyTorch to audio processing tasks. It offers tools for feature extraction, data augmentation, and access to popular datasets. Whether you're working on speech recognition or audio classification,

TorchAudio provides a foundation for your projects.

```python
import torchaudio

# Example: Loading an audio file
waveform, sample_rate = torchaudio.load('path/to/audio/file.wav', normalize=True)
```

d. Ignite: A High-Level Training Framework

Ignite simplifies the training and evaluation of PyTorch models. It provides abstractions for common training tasks, making it easier to experiment with different architectures and hyperparameters. Ignite's simplicity and extensibility make it a valuable asset in your deep learning toolkit.

```python
from ignite.engine import Events,
create_supervised_trainer,
create_supervised_evaluator

# Example: Creating a simple trainer and evaluator
trainer = create_supervised_trainer(model,
optimizer, loss_fn)
```

```python
evaluator = create_supervised_evaluator(model,
metrics={'accuracy': Accuracy()})
```

e. PyTorch Hub: Sharing Models and Components

PyTorch Hub serves as a platform for sharing pre-trained models, components, and utilities. It simplifies model deployment by providing a centralized repository for the PyTorch community to share and discover resources.

```python
# Example: Loading a pre-trained model from PyTorch Hub
```

```
import torch.hub

model = torch.hub.load('pytorch/vision:v0.11.0',
'resnet18', pretrained=True)
```
` ` `

f. Fastai: Deep Learning Simplified

Fastai is a high-level deep learning library built on top of PyTorch. It emphasizes simplicity and ease of use, enabling rapid development of models for various tasks. Fastai's integrated approach to training models and handling data makes it a favorite among both beginners and experienced practitioners.

```python
from fastai.vision.all import *


# Example: Creating a simple image classification
model with Fastai
dls = ImageDataLoaders.from_folder('path/to/data',
valid_pct=0.2)
learn = cnn_learner(dls, resnet34, metrics=accuracy)
```

Embrace the PyTorch Ecosystem:

The PyTorch ecosystem is a thriving and collaborative space, continually evolving with contributions from researchers and developers worldwide. As you navigate through the diverse libraries and frameworks, leverage the collective knowledge of the PyTorch community to accelerate your journey in deep learning and artificial intelligence. Whether you're exploring computer vision, natural language processing, or audio applications, PyTorch's ecosystem has you covered. Dive in, experiment, and join the vibrant community shaping the future of deep learning.

11.2 Community Contributions

In the ever-expanding realm of PyTorch, community contributions stand as the lifeblood that fuels innovation, learning, and collective progress. Let's delve into the diverse and impactful ways in which the PyTorch community contributes to the growth and dynamism of this open-source deep learning framework.

a. GitHub Repositories: A Tapestry of Ideas

PyTorch's GitHub repositories are the epicenter of collaboration. Developers worldwide actively contribute to core PyTorch, as well as numerous community-driven projects. From cutting-edge research implementations to practical utilities, the repositories reflect the shared passion for advancing the capabilities of PyTorch.

Explore repositories on [PyTorch GitHub](https://github.com/pytorch) to uncover a tapestry of ideas, ranging from model architectures to tools that streamline development workflows.

b. Forums and Discussion Platforms: Knowledge Exchange

PyTorch boasts vibrant forums and discussion platforms where developers, researchers, and enthusiasts converge to share insights, seek help, and discuss the latest trends. Platforms like the [PyTorch Discussion Forum](https://discuss.pytorch.org/) and [Stack Overflow](https://stackoverflow.com/questions/tagged/pytorch) serve as hubs for knowledge exchange, troubleshooting, and collaboration.

Engage with the community, ask questions, and contribute by sharing your experiences and expertise.

c. PyTorch Scholarships and Initiatives: Nurturing Talent

PyTorch actively supports initiatives that nurture talent and promote diversity in the field of deep learning. Scholarships, workshops, and mentorship programs, such as the [PyTorch Scholarship Challenge](https://www.udacity.com/scholarships/pytorch), provide learning opportunities and resources to aspiring practitioners.

Explore these initiatives to enhance your skills, connect with mentors, and be part of a supportive learning ecosystem.

d. PyTorch Conferences and Events:

Gathering Minds

PyTorch conferences and events bring together minds from academia and industry to share research breakthroughs, discuss best practices, and explore the latest advancements. Conferences like [PyTorch DevCon](https://pytorch.org/events/2022/devcon 2022/) offer a platform for networking, learning, and staying abreast of the cutting-edge developments in the PyTorch landscape.

Participate in these events to expand your network, gain insights, and contribute to the collective knowledge pool.

e. Educational Resources: Empowering Learners

The PyTorch community actively contributes to educational resources that empower learners at all levels. From blog posts and tutorials to video content, these resources cover a spectrum of topics, making deep learning accessible to a broader audience.

Explore platforms like [PyTorch Tutorials](https://pytorch.org/tutorials/) and [Towards Data Science](https://towardsdatascience.com/tagged/

pytorch) for educational content that suits your learning preferences.

Unleash the Power of Collaboration:

The PyTorch community thrives on the principle of collaboration, where each contribution, no matter how small, adds value to the collective knowledge base. Engage with the community, contribute your expertise, and embark on a journey of continuous learning and innovation. The PyTorch community is not just a group of developers; it's a global force shaping the future of deep learning. Join the conversation, share your insights, and be part of this dynamic ecosystem.

As we conclude our exploration of Chapter 11, it's evident that the PyTorch ecosystem and community are dynamic forces that elevate the framework beyond mere code. PyTorch isn't just a collection of libraries; it's a collaborative journey that weaves together developers, researchers, educators, and learners into a vibrant tapestry of innovation.

From the robust libraries and frameworks like TorchVision and TorchText that extend PyTorch's capabilities to the diverse contributions and discussions flourishing on platforms like GitHub and forums, PyTorch is a testament to the power of open-source collaboration.

The PyTorch community isn't bound by geographical borders; it's a global network of minds connected by a shared passion for advancing deep learning. Whether you're a seasoned researcher pushing the boundaries of AI or a newcomer taking the first steps, the PyTorch community provides an inclusive and supportive environment.

As you navigate through the rich ecosystem, don't just consume; contribute. Your ideas, questions, and experiences are valuable. Engage in discussions, explore the wealth of educational resources, and participate in events that bring the community together.

In this ever-evolving landscape, PyTorch is not just a tool; it's a community-driven force shaping the future of artificial intelligence. Embrace the spirit of collaboration, share your knowledge generously, and together, let's continue pushing the boundaries of what's possible in the exciting world of PyTorch.

CHAPTER 12:
CUTTING-EDGE
DEVELOPMENTS

12.1 PyTorch Lightning: Illuminating Simplicity in Deep Learning

In the ever-evolving landscape of deep learning, PyTorch Lightning emerges as a powerful framework, simplifying the complexities of model training, research, and deployment. Let's delve into the illuminating world of PyTorch Lightning, exploring its key features, benefits, and how it reshapes the way we approach deep learning.

Understanding PyTorch Lightning:

PyTorch Lightning is not just another deep learning library; it's a lightweight wrapper that abstracts away the boilerplate code, enabling researchers and practitioners to focus on the core aspects of their experiments. Born out of the need for cleaner, more organized code in PyTorch projects, Lightning provides a higher-level interface without sacrificing flexibility.

Key Features:

1. Lightweight Structure:

- PyTorch Lightning streamlines the training loop, reducing the code needed for typical tasks. This simplicity enhances readability and makes experimentation more fluid.

2. Reproducibility:

- Lightning ensures reproducibility by standardizing training procedures. With a consistent interface, experiments become easier to share, reproduce, and iterate upon.

3. Flexibility with PyTorch:

- While providing high-level abstractions, Lightning seamlessly integrates with PyTorch. Users retain the flexibility to customize and extend their models, training loops, and evaluation processes.

How PyTorch Lightning Reshapes Workflows:

a. Organized Code Structure:

- Lightning enforces a standardized project structure, promoting code organization. The separation of concerns into LightningModules and the lightning-specific callbacks enhances clarity.

```python
class MyLightningModel(pl.LightningModule):
    def __init__(self):
        super(MyLightningModel, self).__init__()
        # Model components defined here

    def forward(self, x):
        # Forward pass logic

    def training_step(self, batch, batch_idx):
        # Training step logic

    def configure_optimizers(self):
```

```
# Optimizer and learning rate scheduler
configuration


# Instantiate and train the model
model = MyLightningModel()
trainer = pl.Trainer(max_epochs=5)
trainer.fit(model, train_dataloader)
` ` `
```

b. Experiment Configuration:

- Lightning abstracts away the minutiae of experiment configuration. Hyperparameters, logging, and distributed training become more straightforward and consistent.

```python
# Experiment configuration with PyTorch Lightning

trainer = pl.Trainer(max_epochs=5, gpus=2,

log_every_n_steps=50)
```

c. Model Checkpointing:

- With Lightning, model checkpointing is seamless. The Trainer class allows for automatic checkpointing, ensuring that the progress of experiments is preserved.

```python
# Model checkpointing in PyTorch Lightning

trainer = pl.Trainer(checkpoint_callback=True)
```

```
```

Why Choose PyTorch Lightning:

1. Efficiency in Experimentation:

- Lightning accelerates the experimentation process by minimizing boilerplate code. Researchers can iterate quickly and focus on refining models.

2. Reproducibility and Collaboration:

- Standardized interfaces enhance reproducibility, making it easier to share and collaborate on experiments. The consistent structure aids in understanding and extending others' work.

3. Community-Driven Development:

- PyTorch Lightning thrives on a vibrant community actively contributing to its growth. Regular updates, tutorials, and a supportive community make adopting Lightning a forward-looking choice.

Getting Started:

To embark on the PyTorch Lightning journey, install the library and begin transitioning your PyTorch projects with ease:

```bash

pip install pytorch-lightning

```

Explore the [PyTorch Lightning documentation](https://pytorch-lightning.readthedocs.io/) for comprehensive guides and examples.

PyTorch Lightning is more than a framework; it's a paradigm shift in how we approach deep learning. It simplifies, organizes, and illuminates the path for both seasoned researchers and newcomers. As we navigate the cutting-edge developments in deep learning, PyTorch Lightning stands as a beacon, guiding us toward a future of efficient, reproducible, and collaborative AI research and development.

12.2 Research Advances: Pushing the Frontiers of PyTorch

In the ever-evolving landscape of deep learning research, PyTorch remains at the forefront, empowering researchers with tools to push the boundaries of what's possible. Let's delve into the realm of research advances within the PyTorch ecosystem, exploring the latest breakthroughs, frameworks, and methodologies that drive innovation.

1. Neural Architecture Search (NAS):

Neural Architecture Search has gained momentum as a powerful approach to automating the design of neural networks. Researchers harness PyTorch's flexibility to implement NAS algorithms, enabling the discovery of architectures tailored to specific tasks.

Example: Implementing a basic NAS algorithm in PyTorch*

```python
# Define a search space
search_space = ...


# Perform neural architecture search
best_architecture = nas_algorithm(search_space)
```

2. Self-Supervised Learning:

Self-supervised learning techniques have emerged as a key research focus, leveraging PyTorch's versatility to explore pre-training models on large unlabeled datasets. By defining pretext tasks, researchers create self-supervised learning pipelines that yield representations beneficial for downstream tasks.

Example: Implementing a self-supervised learning pipeline*

```python
# Define pretext task
pretext_task = ...


# Create self-supervised learning pipeline
self_supervised_model                                    =
self_supervised_pipeline(pretext_task)
```

3. Transformers and Attention Mechanisms:

The ubiquity of Transformers and attention mechanisms in natural language processing and computer vision research showcases PyTorch's adaptability. Researchers implement novel attention mechanisms, transformer architectures, and transformer-based models to achieve state-of-the-art results.

Example: Implementing a custom attention mechanism in PyTorch*

```python
```

```
# Define a custom attention mechanism

class CustomAttention(nn.Module):

    ...


# Integrate custom attention into a transformer model

transformer_with_custom_attention = TransformerModel(attention=CustomAttention())
```
` ` `

4. Generative Adversarial Networks (GANs):

Advancements in Generative Adversarial Networks continue to shape the landscape of generative modeling. Researchers harness

PyTorch to develop and experiment with novel GAN architectures, exploring applications in image synthesis, style transfer, and beyond.

Example: Implementing a conditional GAN in PyTorch

```python
# Define a conditional GAN model
conditional_gan = ConditionalGAN()
```

5. Federated Learning:

Federated Learning, a paradigm for training models across decentralized devices, has gained prominence. PyTorch's federated learning frameworks enable researchers to explore secure and efficient model training in distributed environments.

Example: Implementing federated learning with PyTorch

```python
# Set up federated learning environment
federated_environment = FederatedEnvironment()
```

```
# Train a model using federated learning
federated_trainer    =    FederatedTrainer(model,
federated_environment)
```

The realm of research advances within the PyTorch ecosystem is a testament to the platform's adaptability and the creativity of the research community. As we explore Neural Architecture Search, Self-Supervised Learning, Transformers, GANs, and Federated Learning, PyTorch serves as the enabler, providing the tools and flexibility needed to turn groundbreaking ideas into reality. The collaborative spirit of the PyTorch community continues to drive innovation, pushing the frontiers of what can be achieved in deep learning research.

As we conclude this comprehensive journey through PyTorch, I extend my sincere gratitude to the readers. From unraveling the fundamentals to exploring cutting-edge developments, this book aims to be your guide in the dynamic realm of deep learning. Thank you for joining this exploration, and may your PyTorch endeavors be filled with innovation and success.

Made in the USA
Las Vegas, NV
07 April 2024

88399260R00295